ITALIAN FOR OPERA LOVERS

Italian *for* Opera Lovers

ALISON OATMAN

OATMAN
BOOKS
Ventura, Cailfornia

To my parents,
Eric and Jane,
for whom the arts were bread and water.

ACKNOWLEDGMENTS

I want to thank my students at the Santa Fe Community College for surviving my classes and providing much-needed input and inspiration. Grazie mille!

CONTENTS

INTRODUCTION

I lucked out with a father who shared his exuberance for the arts with me. While my mother and I cherished her favorite Bob Dylan albums and Fellini films, thanks to my father, I attended many plays, concerts, and operas during my youth spent in Lower Manhattan.

I was a nervous kid. The program stuck to my sweaty palms like flypaper, but I was where I belonged in the audience, more myself in the dark than in the unforgiving light of day. Only in the darkened theater was I truly myself…breathing, pulsating, larger than life. Able to taste the freedom other kids had as they joined life head-on.

Courageous enough to relax my guard and enter the bodies of the singers who sang their lines to thunderous applause, or wiped away a tear, or whispered a melody. Emboldened by the stage to imagine my own boots creaking on the floorboards. There is nothing short of the sheer magic that occurs when just the right scene is lit up and the words hover in the air like poetry.

I was blessed once again when I spent the summer between my junior and senior years of high school with a host family in Italy. My host father, Aimone, played the trumpet and was so much of an opera fan that he named his daughters Carmen and Palmira. Every morning at dawn, my Italian mother Anna put the sauce on the stove in preparation for our daily **pranzo**. Aimone—who worked nearby at a paper factory—would return for two hours at the middle of the day. We would have a meal of many courses and then take a quick **pisolino** upstairs in our bedrooms. Though I was already a vegetarian, I ate everything offered to me that summer, including tins of beef chunks suspended in gelatin. I was terrified of being an ungrateful guest.

Shortly after college, where I majored in Italian, I fell in with a group of "opera friends." We would vamp up every weekend and attend standing room at the Metropolitan Opera, tossing our heels off as soon as we arrived at the burgundy velvet-covered wall that we had to lean against for hours at a time. Then there was the long subway ride home, during which I dozed between stations, exhausted, yet giddy from the music and the spectacle.

Fast forward over twenty years, and I have taught "Italian for Opera Lovers" for two summers in a row at the Santa Fe Community College. The class has been geared to cover two Italian operas on the repertoire each year at the Santa Fe Opera. Sometimes I have wondered about the logic of presenting vocabulary and grammar in a somewhat haphazard way. Yet I find a great deal of pleasure in uniting two great joys in life: the Italian language and opera. I think these two passions are bottom-less—infinitely satisfying. It feels like the journey has just begun.

Let's start by warming up our voices like bonafide opera singers.

VOWELS
Letters/Pronunciation/As in…/Examples

a	ah	bah	banana (bah-NAH-nah)
e	eh	bet	breve (BREH-veh)
i	eeh	beet	vino (VEE-noh)
o	oh	bought	moto (MOH-toh)
u	ooh	boot	fumo (FOO-moh)

ALPHABET
Lettera Pronuncia   Parola

a	a	aereo
b	bi	bicicletta
c	ci	cinema
d	di	dentro

e	e	esame
f	effe	fare
g	gi	gatto
h	acca	hamburger
i	i	inverno
l	elle	latte
m	emme	madre
n	enne	nome
o	o	orologio
p	pi	pane
q	cu	qui
r	erre	rosso
s	esse	studente
t	ti	televisione
u	u	università
v	vu	vero
z	zeta	zio

The following letters are only used with foreign words:
le lettere straniere (foreign letters)

j	i lunga	jeep
k	cappa	ketchup
w	doppia vu	western
x	ics	fax
y	ipsilon	yogurt

Saying Hello and Goodbye

Americans are a notoriously casual people. We feel comfortable saying "Hi!" to everyone from our children and our mothers, to our doctors, our professors, our lawyers, and even the local greengrocer. We seldom show a special respect for older people whom we may know well, but who don't belong to our family. Nor do we give much deference to strangers. And we rarely use titles such as "Sir" or "Ma'am," "Professor" or "Doctor" when we come across someone on the street.

Things are a little different in Italy. One would never say **ciao** to a neighbor (especially an older one) or to a boss or to a clerk in a store. And one would certainly never use **ciao** when speaking on the phone to a stranger.

Instead, it's correct to use **buongiorno** (good day) or **buonasera** (good evening) depending on the time of day, and then add a title such as **Signora** (Madam), **Signore** (Sir), **professore** (male professor) **professoressa** (female professor), **dottore** (male doctor), or **dottoressa** (female doctor).

(However, please steer clear of **Signorina** or "Miss"! It's a term for unmarried women of any age that has become discouraged in contemporary Italian.)

For example, one would say, "Buongiorno, Signora!" or "Buonasera, professore!"

There is a lot of debate as to when one switches from **buongiorno** to **buonasera** and conventions vary from region to region. As a general rule, one should switch at lunchtime. Because Romans take their midday meal later than their compatriots in the northern cities, one would still say **buongiorno** in Rome late into the afternoon. **Buonanotte** (good night) is only used right before bed.

Ciao comes from Venetian dialect, where the greeting **s-ciào vostro** meant "I am your slave." It gradually began to be used to mean "I'm at your service" when addressing people of one's own age or older. The term morphed into **s-ciào** and then to **ciao**. I found a source that claims **ciao** was never used as an informal greeting before the 20th century.

If you want to be polite without being overly formal, use the term **salve**. It comes from the Latin verb **salvere** ("to be well, to be in good health"). However, unlike **ciao**, **salve** can only be used as a salutation and cannot be used when parting.

The informal **tu** form is only used with family, friends, children and animals. That means one would use the polite **Lei** form for everyone else—including the fruit seller you see every day, your instructor, and the man at the corner **bar** who prepares your **caffè** each morning.

A Menu of Responses to "How are you?"

When we say, "How are you?" to someone in the United States, it's more of a greeting than a probing inquiry into someone's mental state. This is not true in Italy! When one says (formally) **Come sta?** or (informally) **Come stai?** the aim is to know the exact answer!

Here is a list of options:
Benissimo! Great!
Va benissimo! Things are going great!
Molto bene, grazie. Very well, thanks.
Sto bene! I'm well.
Va bene. Things are going well.
Va tutto bene. Everything's going well.
Abbastanza bene, grazie. Pretty well, thanks.
Così così. So so.
Non c'è male. Not bad.
Non mi posso lamentare. I can't complain.
Insomma. Not too bad.
Non sto bene; Sto male. I'm not well.
Va male. Things aren't going well.
Malissimo! Not well at all!

If someone gives an answer below **Non c'è male**, your mission is to ask **Cosa c'è?** or "What's the matter?" Be prepared for a detailed account! And then it's that person's turn to thank you (**grazie!**) and ask how you are doing (by using either the informal **E tu?** or the formal **E Lei?**).

CHAPTER ONE

George Frideric Handel
(1685-1759)

Handel was born on February 23, 1685 in Halle, Germany, in the same year as both Johann Sebastian Bach and the Italian composer Domenico Scarlatti. His father was dead set on his son becoming a lawyer and therefore he outlawed any musical instruments in the house. As legend has it, young George Frideric would sneak up to the attic each night to play the clavichord in secret while the family slept. Several years later, the budding musician was tooling around on the organ after church one Sunday when a duke overheard him and immediately begged his father not to "rob the world of a rising genius!"

After spending time pursing his music in Hamburg and Italy, Handel arrived in London in his mid-twenties and remained there until his death at the age of seventy-four. Handel wasn't a colorful character. It seems he took little interest in sex or the politics of his day. Books about him make for some particularly juiceless reading. But as anyone familiar with his oratorio *Messiah* can certainly attest, his inner life must have been spectacular.

Handel's Italian operas followed the typical **opera seria** guidelines: the **da capo aria** (A-B-A form) that brought its singer right back to the beginning, over and over again, not to lengthen the lines but to fill them in with more and more vocal acrobatics; the **recitativo secco** or

secco recitative—a dry speaking voice designed to take on the beats of a natural conversation, with the goal of advancing the plot and with the accompaniment of a harpsichord; the conventions of exit and entrance; cross-dressing and castrati; lavish sets calling for cages of canaries, decorated scenery and special effects; and fantastical plots that featured magic and mythological happenings. Ensembles were rare to non-existent.

Three hundred years after Handel started composing, we have a major revival. In fact, recently I caught a performance of *Alcina* at the Santa Fe Opera House.

As I settled into my seat, I thought about all the ways opera has changed since Handel's time. For example, in Handel's day there was no recessed orchestra such as Richard Wagner introduced, allowing the singers to not have to compete for attention with a thundering troupe of instrumentalists.

Also, we now have relatively quiet audiences who are primly attentive. Not so in the eighteenth-century, when it was likely that your neighbor would be munching on a crumbly snack of bread and cheese, talking loudly about whatever crossed his mind, playing games of chess, gambling...not to mention the hanky-panky in the *loges grillés* (shuttered boxes). The opera was just background noise for one's social activities.

Another change is the lack of castrati singers today. As women were shut out of singing in church, the practice of castrating young boys before they reached puberty (usually at the age of eight or nine) became quite popular in Italy. **Evviva il coltello!** (Long live the knife!) audiences would shout after a particularly winning vocal feat by a castrato. It was a way for the young boys to escape poverty. Famous castrati such as Senesino and Farinelli were feted like modern-day celebrities.

What's more, the candle-lit auditoriums were a way of seeing and being seen. Now we take it for granted that most of the theater is dark during the performance—something author Gaia Servadio in her biography of Rossini noted was thanks to scene designer Alessandro Sanquirico (1777-1849), not Wagner as it is commonly claimed. But we can thank

Wagner for his widespread efforts to take away any distractions from the experience of the opera at hand.

These days we have electronic titles, whereas in eighteenth-century London, dual-language librettos were for sale.

Other things that didn't exist back then: epic lines for the ladies' room, women playing roles meant for castrati, the production of an opera that wasn't brand-new and (with that) cerebral reinterpretations of past works to make them fresh again, and (at least in Santa Fe) the blanketing sound of crickets. What doesn't exist now: the sorts of exotic sets that introduced animals onstage (sort of a Noah's Ark), and the most treasured possession of the opera snob: the lorgnette.

Alcina is one of the three operas Handel based on Ariosto's epic poem *Orlando Furioso*—the others being *Orlando* and *Ariodante*. *Alcina* marked the end of Handel's string of successes with Italian operas—a winning streak that had begun in 1710 when he arrived in London. After its initial performance at Covent Garden on April 16, 1735, *Alcina* was produced at least eighteen times before it fell out of favor. It wasn't until 1957 that the opera experienced a comeback with Joan Sutherland in the title role.

As you might expect, the plot is fantastical, as it takes place on Alcina's enchanted island, where she seduces men and then transforms them into stones, animals, plants and waves, among other natural phenomena. It begins with Bradamante who is dressed up like her brother Riccardo so she can seek out her betrothed Ruggiero, who is deeply under the spell Alcina has cast on him. Alcina's sister Morgana immediately falls in love with Bradamante. Ruggiero thinks Alcina is also in love with Bradamante (whom he doesn't recognize), so Alcina vows to turn her into an animal to prove to Ruggiero that she loves him the most. Melisso—Bradamante's tutor—lets Ruggiero wear the magic ring that shows Alcina's enchanted island for what it really is—a barren desert inhabited by monsters.

Ruggiero sings his famous aria *Verdi prati* ("Green Meadows")—his farewell to the island whose former beauty will remain forever in his heart. Ruggiero reunites with Bradamante and they plot to escape Alcina's clutches, only for Alcina's magic powers to dissolve away in the face of her true love for Ruggiero.

Oberto—a young man who has spent the opera searching for his father—is tricked by Alcina into almost killing a lion. At the last moment, he recognizes his father's face in the animal's features and stops himself just in time.

Finally, Alcina sings a heartbroken wail of an aria in which she hopes for oblivion. Bradamante and Ruggiero destroy the source of Alcina's magic (usually represented by an urn) and the magic palace turns into dust. Alcina and Morgana sink into the ground, while Alcina's former lovers (including Oberto's father) are returned to their true selves. Everyone sings of relief and happiness.

Alcina (1735)
O s'apre al riso (Morgana, Act I)

In this first scene, Morgana (Alcina's sister) falls in love at first sight (she experiences what in Italian is called **un colpo di fulmine**) with Bradamante (disguised as her own brother).

> **O s'apre al riso**
> **O parla, o tace,**
> **Ha un non so che**
> **Il tuo bel viso,**
> **Che troppo piace**
> **Caro, al mio cor.**

Whether it smiles, (literally, "whether it opens itself to a smile")
Or speaks, or is silent,
Your handsome face
Has a certain quality
Which is only too pleasing
Beloved, to my heart.

VOCABULARY

il riso: laughter
il riso e il pianto: laughter and tears

Not to be confused with:
il riso: rice
il riso integrale: brown rice

parla: he/she speaks
parlare: to speak

Present tense conjugation of parlare:	
(io) parlo	I speak
(tu) parli	you (singular) speak
(lui/lei/Lei) parla	he/she/you (formal) speaks
(noi) parliamo	we speak
(voi) parlate	you (plural) speak
(loro) parlano	they speak

Parla inglese? Do you (formal) speak English?
la parola: speech, word
una parola difficile: a difficult word

un non so che: a quality that cannot be described or named easily:
un je ne sais quoi

il tuo bel viso: your beautiful face
il viso: face
la crema per il viso: face cream

troppo: too much
troppo poco: too little

caro, a: dear
mio caro, mia cara: my dear
Cara signora! My dear lady!

il cor/il cuore: heart
una persona di buon cuore: a kind-hearted soul
senza cuore: heartless
parlare col cuore in mano: to speak frankly

Questo è il cielo di contenti (Chorus, Act I)

In this scene, the chorus representing Alcina's magic island sings with joy.

> **Coro (chorus):**
> **Questo è il cielo di contenti,**
> **Questo è il centro di goder;**
> **Qui è l'Eliso de' viventi,**
> **Qui l'eroe forma il piacer.**

This is the paradise of satisfaction,
This is the hub of pleasure;
Here are the Elysian fields of the living,
Here the hero takes his leisure.

VOCABULARY

questo: this

questo è troppo! This is too much! or This is the limit!

È: he/she/it is

Not to be confused with:

e: and

io e te: me and you

essere: to be

sono: I am

sono francese: I am French

sono americano, a: I am American

sono un ragazzo italiano: I am an Italian boy

non sono canadesi: They are not Canadian.

È un esercizio facile: It's an easy exercise.

Noi siamo stanchi; voi siete stanchi? We are tired; are you tired?

Present tense conjugation of essere	
(io) sono	I am
(tu) sei	you (singular) are
(lui, lei, Lei) è	he/she/you (formal) is
(noi) siamo	we are
(voi) siete	you (plural) are
(loro) sono	they are

il cielo: sky or heaven

un cielo azzurro: a blue sky

Santo cielo! Good heavens!

contento, a: happy, glad
sono contento di vederti: I'm happy to see you (informal)

il centro: center
il centro commerciale: shopping center

godere: to enjoy
godersi la vita: to enjoy life
Gode di buona salute: She enjoys good health.

qui: here
vieni qui: come here

Eliso: Elysium

il piacere: pleasure
i piaceri della vita: the pleasures of life
È un piacere averti qui: it's a pleasure to have you here
È un viaggio d'affari o di piacere? Is this trip for business or for pleasure?
per piacere/per cortesia/per favore: three ways of saying "please"
Mi piace la pizza: I like pizza
Mi piacciono questi ragazzi: I like these boys

mi piace/mi piacciono: If the person or thing you like is singular, you use **mi piace.** If the person or thing you like is plural, use **mi piacciono.** For example, **Mi piace l'Italia!** (I like Italy!), but **Mi piacciono le scarpe!** (I like shoes!)

Remember that in Italy, people don't say "I love pizza!" (**Amo la pizza!**), unless they are planning to seduce a cheese pie. Instead, you would say **Mi piace la pizza!** (or, literally, "Pizza is pleasing to me!").

Di', cor mio quanto t'amai (Alcina, Act I)

Here, Alcina is encouraging Ruggiero to tell the visitors of her love for him.

Di' cor mio, quanto t'amai,
Mostra il bosco, il fonte, il rio,
Dove tacqui e sospirai,
Pria di chiederti mercè.
Dove fisso ne' miei rai,
Sospirando, al sospir mio,
Mi dicesti con uno sguardo,
Peno, ed ardo al par di te.

Tell them, my heart, how much I loved you,
Show them the wood, the spring, the river,
Where I fell silent and sighed,
Before begging your pity.
Where, transfixed by my eyes,
Sighing in answer to my sighs,
You told me with a look.
I suffer and burn as you do.

VOCABULARY

amare: to love
Ti amo: I love you
Mi ami? Do you love me?

Not to be confused with:
Ti voglio bene: I love you (family, friends)
Volersi bene: to love (family and friends)

il bosco: the woods, the forest

il fonte: the spring

Not to be confused with:
la primavera: spring (season)

OTHER NATURE VOCABULARY:
il mare: the sea
il fiume: the river
la collina: the hill
la montagna: the mountain

il cielo: the sky
il sole: the sun
la luna: the moon
la nuvola: the cloud
il vento: the wind

Piove! It's raining!
Tuona! It's thundering!
Nevica! It's snowing!

chiederti: to ask you
chiedere: to ask
ho chiesto il conto al cameriere: I asked the waiter for the check
ti chiedo scusa: I apologize to you

Chi m'insegna il caro padre? (Oberto, Act I)

Here is young Oberto, looking for his lost father.

> **Chi m'insegna il caro padre?**
> **Chi mi rende il genitor?**
> **Per far lieto questo cor?**
> **M'abbandona la speranza**
> **Langue in me bella costanza;**
> **Agitato è in me l'amor.**

> Who will find my dear father?
> Who will restore him to me?
> And lighten this heart?
> Hope deserts me;
> Fair constancy grows faint within me;
> My love is in turmoil.

VOCABULARY
la famiglia: the family
il padre: the father
la madre: the mother
i genitori: the parents

Not to be confused with:
il parente/la parente: relative
i nostri parenti: our relatives

il figlio: the son
la figlia: the daughter
Quanti figli avete? How many children do you have?

il fratello: the brother
la sorella: the sister

il nonno: the grandfather
la nonna: the grandmother

lo zio: the uncle
la zia: the aunt

il nipote/la nipote: grandchild or nephew/niece

il cugino/la cugina: cousin

la moglie: the wife
il marito: the husband

lieto, a: happy
molto lieto (di fare la sua conoscenza): pleased to meet you (formal)

la speranza: hope

Di te mi rido (Ruggiero, Act I)

Ruggiero is desperate to find Alcina.

> **Di te mi rido, semplice stolto.**
> **Sieguo Cupido, amo un bel volto.**
> **Nè so mancar di fè.**
> **Il caro bene che m'innamora**
> **A me non viene?**
> **Non torna ancora? Che fa?**
> **Dov'è? ancor non torna?**

You make me laugh, simple fool.
I follow Cupid, I love a fair face.
I cannot be lacking in faith.
The dear being who inspires me with love
Does not come to me?
Has she not come back? What is she doing?
Where is she? Is she still not back?

VOCABULARY

Di te mi rido: I laugh at you/I make fun of you.
ridere: to laugh
sorridere: to smile

A me non viene? Does she not come to me?
Non torna ancora? or **Ancor non torna?** Has she not returned yet?
Che fa? What is she doing?
Dov'è? Where is she?

How to Ask Questions in Italian

How do you pose a question in Italian? Italian interrogative words mean the same as they do in English: who, what, when, where, why, and how (the classic journalism questions!). By knowing basic Italian interrogatives, you'll be able to express your questions, even without mastery of a long list of vocabulary.

For example, say you're at an Italian street market and you want to buy a beautiful antique bracelet of white and yellow gold. If you know enough vocabulary, you could say **Quanto è questo braccialetto in oro bianco e giallo?** (How much is this bracelet of white and yellow gold?). But if you don't know the correct words, you can also point to the bracelet and simply say **Quanto è?** and the seller will understand that you want to know the price.

- **Chi?** Who?
- **Che? Cosa?** Che cosa? What?
- **Quando?** When?
- **Dove?** Where?
- **Perchè?** Why?
- **Come?** How?
- **Quanto? Quanta? Quanti? Quante?** How much? How many?
- **Quale?** Which?
- **C'è?** or **Ci sono?** Is there? Are there?
- **Cosa c'è?** means "What is there?" but it can also mean, "What's wrong?"

You may also form questions simply by changing the tone of your voice and adding a slight lilt at the end. For example, **Avete mangiato bene** (You ate well.) becomes **Avete mangiato bene?** (Did you eat well?).

Get into the habit of beginning your sentences with **scusi** (formal) or **scusa** (informal), and then adding **per favore** or **per cortesia** at the end.

Some useful phrases:
Scusi. Parla inglese? Excuse me. Do you speak English? (formal)
Scusa. Parli inglese? Excuse me, do you speak English? (informal)

Me lo traduce, per cortesia? Will you translate it for me, please? (formal)
Me lo traduci, per cortesia? Will you translate it for me, please? (informal)

Può parlare più lentamente? Can you speak more slowly? (formal)
Puoi parlare più lentamente? Can you speak more slowly? (informal)

Può ripetere, per favore? Can you please repeat that? (formal)
Puoi ripetere, per favore? Can you please repeat that? (informal)

Chi è? Who is it?
Altro? Anything else?
Desidera altro? Would you like anything else?

Pronto! Chi parla? Hello! Who's speaking? (When answering your phone...)

Che cosa è questo? What is this?

Cosa fai? What are you doing?

Com'è quel ristorante? How's that restaurant?

C'è un problema? Is there a problem?

Dov'è un Bancomat? Where is an ATM machine?

Dov'è la stazione? Where is the train station?

Può mostrarmi dov'è? Can you show me where it is? (formal)

Quale strada devo prendere? Which street should I take?

Scusi/Scusa. Dov'è il bagno? Excuse me. Where is the bathroom?

Dove si trova il museo? Where is the museum?

A che ora bisogna lasciare la camera? What is checkout time?

A che ora chiudete? What time do you close?

Dov'è il mercato coperto? Where is the covered market?

Quanto? How much?

Quanto costa? Quanto è? How much does it cost?

Scusi, che prezzo fa questo? Excuse me, how much is this?

Che orario fate? What are the store's hours?

To turn a sentence into a question, sometimes you need to reverse the word order and place the subject at the end of the sentence. For example, **Gli studenti sono bravi** (The students are smart) becomes **Sono bravi gli studenti?** (Are the students smart?). And **Maria è italiana** (Maria is Italian) becomes **È italiana, Maria?** (Is Maria Italian?).

Verdi prati, selve amene (Ruggiero, Act II)

Here is the most famous aria in the opera. Ruggiero sings nostalgically of the beauty of the island, which he now sees as a desert.

Verdi prati, selve amene,
Perderete la beltà.
Vaghi fior, correnti rivi,
La vaghezza, la bellezza,
Presto in voi si cangerà.
E cangiato il vago oggetto,
All'orror del primo aspetto
Tutto in voi ritornerà.

Green meadows, pleasant woods,
You will lose your beauty.
Lovely flowers, flowing rivers,
Your charm and beauty
Will soon change.
And with the change of the lovely place,
To the horror of its former appearance
Everything in you will return.

VOCABULARY

verde: green
gli anni verdi: the green years (youth)
verde pisello: pea green

i campi: fields
le selve: the woods
ameno, a: pleasant

la bellezza: beauty
un istituto di bellezza: a beauty salon
Che bellezza! Fantastic!
Ciao bellezza! Hello gorgeous!

presto: soon, quickly, early
a presto: see you soon
fai presto! hurry up!
mi alzo sempre presto: I always get up early

Ma quando tornerai (Alcina, Act III)

"When you come back…you'll be sorry!" Alcina warns Ruggiero.

Ma quando tornerai
Di lacci avvinto il piè,
Attendi pur da me
Rigore e crudeltà.
E pur, perchè t'amai,
Ho ancor di te pietà.
Ancor placar mi puoi,
Mio ben, cor mio; non vuoi?
Mi lascia, infido, e va!

But when you come back
With your feet in chains,
Expect only from me
Harshness and cruelty.
And yet, because I loved you,
I still have pity on you.

You can still placate me,
My love, my heart; do you not wish to go?
Leave me, faithless man, go!

VOCABULARY

ma: but, yet, still

ti dispiace? ma no! Do you mind? Of course not!

quando: when

quando vai in vacanza? When are you going on vacation?

tornerai: you will come back

tornare: to come back

tornare a casa: to go home

A che ora torni da scuola? What time do you get home from school?

ho ancor di te pietà: I still have pity on you

ho: I have

avere: to have

ancora: still

ancora oggi: still today

non ancora: not yet

pietà: pity

ancor placar mi puoi: you can still placate me

ancora: still

placare: calm down, pacify, to soothe

puoi: you (sing) can

Mio ben, cor mio; non vuoi? My love, my heart; do you not wish to?

bene: well, properly

sto bene: I'm fine

va bene: all right, okay

il mio bene: my love

il mio cuore: my heart

vuoi: you (sing) want

non vuoi: you don't want

Mi lascia, infido, e va! Leave me, faithless man, go!

mi lascia: leave me

infido, a: treacherous

e va! And go!

andare: to go

andare a casa: to go home

Present tense conjugation of andare

(io) vado	I go
(tu) vai	you (singular) go
(lui, lei, Lei) va	he/she/you (formal) goes
(noi) andiamo	we go
(voi) andate	you (plural) go
(loro) vanno	they go

Chapter Two

Wolfgang Amadeus Mozart
(1756-1791)

Mozart's love of jokes and puns and his galloping passion for dancing would have made him a lively dinner companion. In fact, he wrote 229 full-scored dances, including 56 German dances. Vienna was in a frenzy about the waltz.

One surprising discovery was the Mozart family's enjoyment of coarse jokes. Mozart's mother wrote to her husband in 1777: "I send greetings to Tresel also and should like you to tell her that it is all one whether I shit the muck or she eats it." In fact, the family's letters are chock full of scatological humor (that I won't repeat here any further)! It's unclear whether this was in vogue at the time or just an eccentricity that belonged to the Mozarts.

Mozart composed twenty-two operas, but his most famous ones— *Le Nozze di Figaro, Don Giovanni,* and *Così Fan Tutte*—sprang from his partnership with the librettist Lorenzo Da Ponte. Da Ponte was born Emanuele Conegliano, the son of a Jewish leatherworker in a small city located in the state of Venice, where fifty Jews lived in a ghetto. (The word "ghetto" comes from **geto**—which meant "old public foundry" in Venetian dialect.) The Jewish men there had to wear red hats, while the women were forced to put on red scarves. They weren't allowed out of the ghetto at night.

In 1763, the Conegliano family (with few options) converted to Christianity. Bishop Da Ponte was delighted to guide them in their new faith and they took on his name. Lorenzo Da Ponte quickly took to learning and acquired an expensive taste for literature in Italian. As the local bookseller's son was a shoemaker who needed leather, they came to an agreement. Lorenzo sneakily stuffed the back of his coat with samples of his father's leather. Just then, his stepmother (only four years older than he was) spotted him. "The poor hunchback!" someone shouted. At this exclamation, the pieces of hide tumbled out and onto the ground. Thanks to his stepmother, his father was summoned right away, and he unleashed his fury on the young Lorenzo. When Bishop Da Ponte heard about this, he was amused and provided the adolescent with money for the books he wanted.

Soon Lorenzo became an abbé so he could continue his studies. Yet the pleasures of Venetian life at the time (including the delights of opera houses) were too seductive. In no time at all, Da Ponte's morals were relaxed and he compromised himself to such a degree that in 1779 he was exiled from Venice for fifteen years.

Once in Vienna, Da Ponte met Mozart and they struck up a good working relationship. After the success of *Le nozze di Figaro*, Da Ponte penned his own verison of the Don Juan story, and he called it *il dissoluto punito, o sia Il Don Giovanni* ("The Rake Punished, or Don Giovanni"). *Don Giovanni* (1787) is neither an **opera seria** (a serious work), nor an **opera buffa** (a funny work)—but a **dramma giocoso** (a playful drama). It is a story about the madness of endless consumption—of women, of food, of drink. The opera begins with a masked Don Giovanni getting chased by Donna Anna out of her bedroom in the dark. Anna's father comes out to protect her, but he is killed by the Don.

Next, we meet Donna Elvira, who has been seduced and abandoned. She is set to get revenge on Don Giovanni, but he slips away. Then there is a wedding party for two peasants: Masetto and Zerlina. Don Giovanni sees a good opportunity to seduce Zerlina. She yields to him.

Donna Anna and her fiancé Don Ottavio unmask Don Giovanni and hold him responsible for his crimes. Finally, after many colorful scenes, Don Giovanni has dinner with the stone statue of the Commendatore (Donna Anna's dead father) and the unrepentant lover is dragged into hell.

As Fred Plotkin points out in his essential guide, *Opera 101*, opera lovers often have sex on the mind and performances can be more erotic than "cheaper" entertainments, such as film or television. Well, Don Giovanni is pure unrelenting Eros. He pursues his female conquests with a wild mania and a lust that can never be satisfied.

Notte e giorno faticar (Leporello, Act I)

Don Giovanni's servant Leporello, in a cloak, pacing up and down in front of Donna Anna's house.

Notte e giorno faticar
Slaving night and day

Per chi nulla sa gradir;
For whom nothing pleases,

Pioggia e vento sopportar,
Enduring rain and wind,

Mangiar male e mal dormir...
Ill fed and short of sleep...

Voglio far il gentiluomo,
I'd like to live the life of a gentleman

E non voglio piu servir.
And serve no more.

Oh, che caro galantuomo!
Oh, what a fine gallant!

Vuol star dentro colla bella,
He likes to be indoors with a beauty

Ed io far la sentinella!
While I keep watch outside!

Ma mi par…che venga gente;
But I think someone's coming…

Non mi voglio far sentir.
I don't want to be seen.

(S'asconde.)
(He hides.)

VOCABULARY

la notte: night
buonanotte: good night (use right before going to bed)
dare la buonanotte: to say goodnight
notte bianca: sleepless night
il giorno: day
che giorno è oggi? What day is it today?

la pioggia: rain
il vento: wind

mangiare: to eat
vuoi mangiare qualcosa? Would you like something to eat?
mangiare come un uccellino: to eat like a bird

dormire: to sleep

voglio: I want
volere: to want

volere è potere: to want (to do something) is to be able (to do something)
certo si può: yes, you can
me la cavo: I'll handle it

Present tense conjugation of volere:

(io) voglio	I want
(tu) vuoi	you (singular) want
(lui, lei, Lei) vuole	he/she/you (formal) wants
(noi) vogliamo	we want
(voi) volete	you (plural) want
(loro) vogliono	they want

---

la gente: people
la donna: woman
le donne: women
l'uomo: man
gli uomini: men

Madamina (Leporello, Act I)

The list of Don Giovanni's conquests.

> **Madamina, il catolago è questo**
> Little lady, this is the list

> **Delle belle che amò il padron mio,**
> Of the beauties my master has loved,

Un catalogo egli e che ho fatt'io,
A list I've made out myself;

Osservate, leggete con me.
Take a look, read it with me.

In Italia seicento e quaranta,
In Italy six hundred and forty,

In Almagna duecento e trent'una,
In Germany two hundred and thirty-one,

Cento in Francia, in Turchia novant'una,
One hundred in France, ninety-one in Turkey,

Ma in Ispagna son già mille e tre.
But in Spain already a thousand and three.

V'han fra queste contadine,
Among them are country girls,

Cameriere e cittadine,
Waiting maids, city beauties;

V'han contesse, baronesse
There are countesses, baronesses,

Marchesane, principesse,
Marchionesses, princesses;

E v'han donne di ogni grado,
Women of every rank,

D'ogni forma, d'ogni età.
Of every size, of every age.

Nella bionda egli ha l'usanza
In a fair girl

Di lodar la gentilezza,
he will praise her kindness,

Nella bruna la costanza,
A dark one's constancy,

Nella bianca la dolcezza.
A white-haired one's sweetness.

Vuol d'inverno la grassotta,
In the winter he prefers them plump,

Vuol' d'estate la magrotta;
In summer, slim;

È la grande maestosa,
He calls a tall one stately,

La piccina è ognor vezzosa...
A tiny one always dainty.

Delle vecchie fa conquista
Even the elderly he courts

Pel piacer di porle in lista;
For the pleasure of adding them to the list;

Sua passion predominante
but his supreme passion

È la giovin principiante.
Is the young beginner.

Non si picca se sia ricca,
He cares not if she's rich

Se sia brutta, se sia bella;
Plain or pretty—

Purchè porti la gonnella,
So long as she wears a skirt,

Voi sapete quel che fa.
You know what his game is!

VOCABULARY

le stagioni: the seasons
la primavera: spring
l'estate: summer
l'autunno: fall, autumn
l'inverno: winter

i mesi: the months
gennaio (jeh-NNAH-yoh): January
febbraio (feh-BBRAH-yoh): February
marzo (MAHR-isoh): March
aprile (ah-PREE-leh): April
maggio (MAH-joh): May
giugno (JOO-nyoh): June
luglio (LOO-llyoh): July
agosto (ah-GOHS-toh): August
settembre (she-TTEHM-breh): September
ottobre (oh-TTOH-breh): October
novembre (noh-VEHM-breh): November
dicembre (dee-CHEHM-breh): December

ADJECTIVES

dolce: sweet, gentle mild
amaro, a: bitter, unpleasant

bello, a: beautiful, handsome
brutto, a: ugly

alto, a: tall
basso, a: short (of stature)

grasso, a: fat
magro, a: thin

biondo, a: blond
castano, a: chestnut-brown
grigio, a: gray
nero, a: black
bianco, a: white
bruno, a: brown

allegro, a: happy
triste: sad

giovane: young
anziano, a: old
vecchio, a: old

debole: weak
forte: strong

attivo, a: active
pigro, a: lazy

ricco, a: rich
povero, a: poor

veloce: fast
lento, a: slow

NATIONALITIES
l'Australia: Australia
australiano, a: Australian

l'Austria: Austria
austriaco, a: Austrian

la Cina: China
cinese: Chinese

la Francia: France
francese: French

la Germania: Germany
tedesco, a: German

il Giappone: Japan
giapponese: Japanese

la Grecia: Greece
greco, a: Greek

l'Inghilterra: England
inglese: English

l'Italia: Italy
italiano, a: Italian

il Messsico: Mexico
messicano, a: Mexican

la Russia: Russia
russo, a: Russian

la Spagna: Spain
spagnolo, a: Spanish

gli Stati Uniti: United States
americano, a: American

la Turchia: Turkey
turco, a: Turkish

NUMBERS

1 **uno**

2 **due**

3 **tre**

4 **quattro** (KWAH-ttroh)

5 **cinque** (CHEEN-kweh)

6 **sei** (SEH-ee)

7 **sette**

8 **otto**

9 **nove**

10 **dieci** (DYEH chee)

11 **undici** (OOHN-dee-chee)

12 **dodici** (DOH-dee-chee)

13 **tredici** (TREH-dee-chee)

14 **quattordici** (kwah-TTOHR-dee-chee)

15 **quindici** (KWEEN-dee-chee)

16 **sedici** (SEH-dee-chee)

17 **diciasette** (dee-chah-SSEH-tteh)

18 **diciotto** (dee-CHOH-ttoh)

19 **diciannove** (dee-chah-NNOH-veh)

20 **venti** (VEHN-tee)

21 **venti + uno=ventuno** (note the dropped vowel)

22 **venti + due=ventidue**

23 **venti + tre=ventitré** (note the accent)

24 **venti + quattro=ventiquattro**

25 **venti + cinque=venticinque**

26 **venti + sei=ventisei**

27 **venti + sette=ventisette**

28 **venti + otto=ventotto** (note the dropped vowel)

29 **venti + nove=ventinove**

30 **trenta**

40 **quaranta**

50 **cinquanta**
60 **sessanta**
70 **settanta**
80 **ottanta**
90 **novanta**
100 **cento**
200 **duecento**
300 **trecento**
1000 **mille**
2000 **duemila** (note the mila form in the plural)
3000 **tremila**
1,000,000 **un milione**
2,000,000 **due milioni**

Finch'han dal vino ("Champagne Aria"; Don Giovanni, Act I)

As fast-moving as a dance…

> **Finch'han dal vino**
> As long as there's wine
>
> **calda la testa**
> to heat one's head
>
> **una grande festa**
> a grand party
>
> **fa preparar!**
> prepare!

Se trovi in piazza
If you find in the town square

qualche ragazza,
some girl,

teco ancor quella
try to bring her

cerca menar.
along too.

Senza alcun ordine
In no set order,

la danza sia,
let there be dancing,

chi'l minuetto,
some the minuet,

chi la follia,
some the follia,

chi l'alemana
some the allemande!

farai ballar!
you get to dance!

Ed io frattanto
And meanwhile,

dall'altra canto,
on the other hand,

con questa e quella
to this girl and that

vo'amoreggiar.
I'll make love.

Ah, la mia lista
Ah, my list

doman mattina
tomorrow morning

d'una decina
by ten or so

devi aumentar!
you must increase!

la ragazza: girl, young woman, girlfriend
una ragazza alta e bionda: a tall blonde girl

è la mia ragazza: she's my girlfriend
brava ragazza: nice girl, good sort

la danza: dancing
la danza classica: ballet dancing

Una grande festa fa preparar!
Prepare for a big party!

VOCABULARY FOR FOOD AND DRINK

Italian Coffee Drinks

Most Italians go to a **bar** (a café) for coffee before work. At most places, you must pay for your coffee before ordering it. As a rule of thumb, it's best to go to the cash register (**la cassa**) first so you can order and pay. Take the receipt (**lo scontrino**) you're given and don't throw it out. Instead, hand it to the barista to get served.

You'll find all sorts of people at the bar: young people, older people, couples, singles, families, business people, students, children and even a customer with a dog. You might see men playing cards if there are tables. You'll also see people buried in the newspaper or simply watching the world pass by.

Un pub is a place to gather in the evenings (in the British tradition) and **un discopub** offers dancing. **Un American bar** is just what it sounds like a traditional bar in the American sense.

Please note that there is an unofficial rule in Italy that one does not order cappuccino after eleven in the morning. At local cafes that aren't used to tourists, you might get a very funny look! One theory is that the milk and the foam make it a meal replacement. Another has it that dairy upsets the digestion. You'll certainly never see an Italian ordering a cappuccino after dinner.

Caffè: This is what we would call espresso—a small cup of very strong coffee topped with **crema** (a caramel-colored foam).

Caffè Hag: A decafinated version. You can order a **decafinato** as well. Hag is the name of the largest producer of Italian decaf coffee and that's the way it is written out on **bar** menu boards.

Caffè lungo: A long coffee—weak and bitter. Also called **caffè americano** (American coffee). Italians refer to it as **acqua sporca** (dirty water)!

Caffè ristretto: A "restricted coffee"—concentrated but not bitter.

Caffè con panna: Espresso with sweet whipped cream.

Caffè con zucchero: Espresso with sugar. In some places—especially in the south around Naples—the coffee comes with sugar and you must order it **senza zucchero** (without sugar) if you don't like it sweet.

Caffè corretto: Coffee "corrected" with a drizzle of liquor, such as sambuca, cognac or grappa.

Caffè macchiato: Coffee "stained" with milk—usually just a spot of foam on top of the espresso.

Caffè latte: Espresso with hot milk—a cappuccino without the foam, usually served in a glass. This is what we call a **latte** in the U.S.—but in Italy don't ask for a **latte,** since you will be served plain milk.

Latte macchiato: Steamed milk "stained" with espresso and served in a glass.

Cappuccino: a shot of espresso in a larger cup with steamed milk and foam.

Bicerìn: Traditional drink of Piemonte around Torino, made of dense hot chocolate, espresso and cream, delicately arranged in a small glass.

Caffè freddo: Iced, or at least cold, coffee.

Caffè d'orzo: Espresso made with barley rather than coffee.

Caffè Shakerato: A sort of Frappuccino that one gets at Starbucks: espresso, sugar, ice, and (sometimes) chocolate syrup, shaken until frothy.

ALSO AT THE LOCAL BAR
il tè: tea
una coca-cola: a Coke
un bicchiere d'acqua minerale: a glass of mineral water
la succa di frutta: fruit juice
la spremuta d'arancia: freshly squeezed orange juice.
l'aranciata: orange soda
la limonata: lemonade
l'acqua tonica: tonic water
l'apertivo: aperitif
il vino: wine
la birra: beer

il cornetto: a croissant
il panino: a bun sandwich

il tramezzino: crustless sandwiches with popular fillings such as tuna, olive, and prosciutto. The origin of the **tramezzino** can be found at the Caffè Mulassano di Piazza Castello in Torino, where it was invented in 1925 as an alternative to English tea sandwiches. The word **tramezzino** was conjured up by the writer Gabriele D'Annunzio as a replacement for the English word "sandwich," being easy to pronounce and entirely Italian. (**Tramezzino** sounds like "in-between," with the addition of the diminutive suffix -ino.)

OTHER VOCABULARY AL BAR
la (prima) colazione: breakfast
il pranzo: lunch
la cena: dinner
uno spuntino: a snack
fare uno spuntino: to have a snack

vorrei: I would like.
vorrei un caffè espresso: I would like an espresso coffee.
per favore: please

subito: right away
altro? anything else?

comprare: to buy
vorrei comprare dieci panini: I would like to buy ten sandwiches
da portare via: to take out

OTHER PLACES TO EAT...
Dove mangiamo? Where are we eating?
il ristorante: a formal place where you eat a first course (**il primo**), a second course (**il secondo**), and a dessert (**il dolce**).
la pizzeria: an informal place that offers primarily pizza
la tavola calda: serves pizza by the slice (**al taglio**) and other prepared dishes

l'osteria: offers wine and beer and simple food
la trattoria: similar to a restaurant but less formal and less expensive

mangiare: to eat
Ti posso offrire qualcosa da mangiare? Can I offer you something to
 eat?
bere: to drink
Che cosa hai bevuto ieri sera? What did you drink last night?

il pane: bread
la pasta: pasta, or (alternatively) a piece of pastry

l'uovo: egg
la farina: flour
lo zucchero: sugar
la carne: meat
il pesce: fish
la verdura: vegetables
l'insalata: salad (greens)
la frutta: fruit
il formaggio: cheese
il burro: butter

il cibo: nourishment; food; dish
Non tocco cibo da tre giorni: I haven't touched food for three days.

fare la spesa: to shop for groceries
il portafoglio: wallet, pocketbook

il mercato: market
Veronica va tutti i giorni al mercato: Veronica goes to the market
 every day

il supermercato: supermarket
il barattolo: can
i surgelati: frozen food

gli spinaci: spinach
il fico: fig
il cocomero: watermelon
il melone: melon
il peperone: pepper
Che peperoni desidera, signora? Quelli rossi, quelli verdi, o quelli gialli? What kind of peppers do you want, madam? Red, green, or yellow?

la pera: pear
la mela: apple
la pesca: peach
l'arancia: orange
l'albicocca: apricot
il ciliegia: cherry
la prugna: plum
il mandarino: mandarin orange, tangerine
la fragola: strawberry

gustare: to taste
maturo, a: ripe

il dolce: cake; sweet
Il panettone è il classico dolce di Natale: Panettone is the traditional Christmas cake.
la panna: cream
il biscotto: cookie

la salumeria: delicatessen shop
il macellaio: butcher
la panetteria: bakery

il vino: wine

Ho già ordinato un quarto di vino rosso: I've already ordered a quarter liter of wine.

il cavatappi: corkscrew
l'apribottiglie: bottle opener

lo spumante: champagne
il brindisi: toast
Facciamo un brindisi alla salute di Maria! Let's drink a toast to Maria's health!
cin cin: here's to you!
ubriaco, a: drunk

il sale: salt
il pepe: pepper
l'aceto: vinegar
l'olio: oil
la noce moscata: nutmeg
l'aglio: garlic
la cipolla: onion
piccante: spicy
salato, a: salty; salted

al ristorante: in a restaurant
riservare: reserve
Faccio riservare un tavolo per sei o per otto persone? Shall I reserve a table for six or for eight people?

la tovaglia: tablecloth
il piatto: plate
il cucchiaio: (soup) spoon
il cucchiaino: teaspoon
la forchetta: fork
il cotello: knife

il menù: menu
prendere: to take, choose
l'appetito: appetite
Buon appetito! Bon appetit

il primo (piatto): first course
Come primo piatto prendo solo una minestra: As a first course, I'll
  just have soup.

il secondo (piatto): second course
le cozze: mussels
la bistecca: steak

il contorno: side dish
E di contorno? And as a side dish?
i fagiolini: green beans
Vorrei dei fagiolini al burro: I would like green beans sautéed
  in butter.

lo stuzzicadenti: toothpick
Cameriere, potrei avere degli stuzzicadenti, per favore? Waiter, can
  you bring me some toothpicks, please?

Other things to keep in mind when eating out…

il cameriere: the waiter
il conto: the bill
un coperto: cover charge
il servizio: service charge
una mancia: a tip
fare alla romana: to split the check in equal parts (i.e., "to go Dutch")

Batti, batti (Zerlina, Act I)

In this, the most cringeworthy of arias, Zerlina asks her newlywed to beat her up for consorting with Don Giovanni on their wedding day.

Batti, batti, o bel Masetto,
Hit, hit, oh handsome Masetto,

la tua povera Zerlina:
your poor Zerlina:

Starò qui come angnellina
I'll stand here like a little lamb

le tue botte ad aspettar.
and await your blows.

Lascerò straziarmi il crine,
I'll let you pull out my hair,

lascerò cavarmi gli occhi;
I'll let you rip out my eyes;

e le care tue manine
and your dear little hands

lieta poi saprò baciar.
then I'll happily kiss.

Ah, lo vedo, non hai core.
Ah, I see, you haven't the heart.

Pace, pace, o vita mia!
Peace, peace, o my life!

In contento ed allegria

In contentment and joy

notte e dì vogliam passar.

we'll spend our nights and days.

VOCABULARY

battere: beat, strike, hit

battersi il petto: to beat one's breast

batteva i denti per il freddo: his teeth were chattering with the cold

battere i piedi: to stamp one's feet

battere i tacchi: to click one's heels

battere le mani: to clap one's hands

povero, a: poor, weak, plain

sono molto poveri: they are very poor

Povera piccola! Poor little thing!

Povera me! Poor me!

agnello: lamb

agnello arrosto: roast lamb

Agnello di Dio: Lamb of God

baciare: to kiss

lo baciò sulla guancia: she kissed him on the cheek

baciarsi: to kiss (each other or one another)

ci siamo baciati: we kissed

l'allegria: cheerfulness, gaiety

Su, un po' di allegria! Come on, cheer up!

Trovi più allegria in un cimitero! You'll find more cheer in a graveyard!

Deh, vieni alla finestra (Don Giovanni, Act II)

The art of seduction and the ultimate serenade.

Deh, vieni alla finestra, o mio tesoro,
O come to my window, my treasure,

Deh, vieni a consolar il pianto mio:
o come and dispel all my sorrow!

Se neghi a me di dar qualche ristoro,
If you refuse me some solace,

Davanti agli occhi tuoi morir vogl'io.
before your eyes I will die.

Tu ch'hai la bocca dolce piu del miele,
Your lips are sweeter than honey,

Tu che il zucchero porti in mezzo al core,
your heart is sweetness itself,

Non esser, gioia mia, con me crudele;
Then be not cruel, my jewel:

Lasciati almen veder, mio bell'amore.
I beg for one glance, my beloved.

V'è gente alla finestra! Forse è dessa:
There's someone at the window, it must be she.

Zì, zì...
Pst! Pst!

VOCABULARY

la finestra: window

il finestrino: small (car/train/plane) window

la vetrina: store window

in vetrina: in the store window

C'è una gonna che mi piace in vetrina: There's a skirt I like in the (store) window.

il tesoro: treasure

Sei un tesoro! How nice of you!

Grazie, tesoro! Thank you, darling!

davanti: in front (of)

davanti c'era un bel giardino: At the front, there was a nice garden.

la casa davanti alla mia: the house opposite mine

Era seduto davanti a me al teatro: He was sitting in front of me at the theater.

dietro: behind, at the back

non guardar dietro: don't look back

la porta di dietro: the back door

la bocca: mouth

rimanere a bocca aperta: to be taken aback

Vuoi chiudere la bocca? Will you shut up?

stare zitto: to shut up

Ti ho detto di stare zitto: I told you to be quiet.

il miele: honey

color miele: honey-colored

crudele: cruel

Non essere così crudele!: Don't be so cruel!

la gente: people
C'era tanta gente: There were lots of people there.
gente di campagna: country people
gente di città: townspeople
È brava gente: They are nice people
Ho gente a cena: I've got people to dinner

forse: perhaps, maybe
Forse hai ragione: Maybe you're right
Verrà? –Forse: Will he come?—Maybe.

Vedrai, carino (Zerlina, Act II)

Here, Zerlina seeks to get back into Masetto's good graces…

Vedrai, carino,
You'll see, my dear,

Se sei buonino,
If you'll be good

Che bel rimedio,
the wonderful cure

Ti voglio dar.
I want to give you.

È naturale,
It's nature's cure

Non dà disgusto,
not unpleasant,

E lo speziale
but no apothecary

Non lo sa far.
Knows how to make it.

È un certo balsamo
It's a certain balm

Che porto addosso:
I carry within me:

Dare te 'l posso,
Which I can give you

Se 'l vuoi provar.
if you'll try it.

Saper vorresti
If you want to know

Dove mi sta?
where I keep it

Sentilo battere,
then feel it beating,

(faccendogli toccar il core)
(making him lay his hand on her heart)

Toccami qua.
Put your hand here.

(Parte con Masetto.)
(She goes off with Masetto.)

VOCABULARY

il rimedio: remedy, cure
un ottimo rimedio contro il raffreddore: an excellent cure for a cold

naturale: natural
È naturale che sia così: It is natural that it should be so.
a grandezza naturale: life-size
i suoi capelli sono biondi naturali: her hair is naturally blond

il disgusto: disgust
dare disgusto: to disgust
lo schifo: disgust
fare schifo: to be disgusting
mi fai schifo: you make me sick

lo speziale: apothecary
lo speziale ha preparato un unguento: the apothecary prepared this
    ointment

Non lo sa far: He doesn't know how to make it
sapere: to know
lo so: I know (it)
Sai nuotare? Do you know how to swim?

conoscere: to know, to be acquainted with, to be familiar with
Non conosco bene la città: I don't know the town well.
conoscere tempi difficili: to go through hard times

il balsamo: balm
il balsamo (per capelli): (hair) conditioner

che porto addosso: that I carry on me
portare: to carry
addosso: on (one's person)
avere addosso: to wear

aveva addosso un vecchio impermeabile: She was wearing an old raincoat

addosso non ho molti soldi: I don't have much money on me

il mio capo mi sta addosso: my boss is breathing down my neck

Speaking of apothecaries, let's talk about Italian pharmacies.

le farmacie: pharmacies

la spazzola: hairbrush

il dentifricio: toothpaste

lo spazzolino da denti: toothbrush

una scatola di fazzolettti di carta: a box of tissues

il rossetto: lipstick/rouge

lo specchio: mirror

il pettine: comb

la lacca per capelli: hairspray

lo smalto per le unghie: nail polish

uno spruzzatore di deodorante: a can of deodorant spray

un rasoio con le lamette: a razor with blades

le aspirine: aspirins

le bende: band-aids

un termometro: a thermometer

To talk about your aches and pains to the pharmacist, use the following formula:

Ho mal di + a body part.

Ho mal di testa. I have a headache.

Ho mal di pancia. I have a stomachache.

Ho mal di gola. I have a sore throat.

la testa: head

la pancia: stomach

la gola: throat

Present tense conjugation of avere	
(io) ho	I have
(tu) hai	you (singular) have
(lui/lei/Lei) ha	he/she/you formal has
(noi) abbiamo	we have
(voi) avete	you (plural) have
(loro) hanno	they have

Expressions with **avere**

avere fame: to be hungry
avere sete: to be thirsty
avere...anni: to be...years old
avere sonno: to be sleepy
avere freddo: to be cold
avere caldo: to be hot
avere paura: to be afraid
avere torto: to be wrong
avere ragione: to be right
avere successo: to be successful
avere bisogno di: to be in need of
avere fretta: to be in a hurry
avere vergogna: to be ashamed
avere voglia di: to want

Mario ha caldo. Mario is hot.
Ugo ha freddo. Ugo is cold.
Maria ha sete. Maria is thirsty.
Sabrina ha fame. Sabrina is hungry.
Giorgio ha sonno. Giorgio is sleepy.
Antonella ha paura. Antonella is afraid.

Luigi ha ragione. Luigi is right.
Silvia ha torto. Silvia is wrong.

To ask someone's age:
Informally: **Quanti anni hai?**
Formally: **Quanti anni ha?**
Answer: **Ho (blank) anni.** For example, **Ho settantacinque anni.**

Marco ha fame. Ha voglia di una pizza.
Marco is hungry. He wants a pizza.

Maria ha sete. Ha bisogno di acqua.
Maria is thirsty. She needs water.

Hai ragione. Luigi ha paura di volare.
You're right. Luigi is afraid of flying.

È inverno. Simona ha freddo.
It's winter. Simona is cold.

È estate. Luca ha caldo.
It's summer. Luca is hot.

È tardi. Serena ha fretta!
It's late. Serena is in a hurry!

CHAPTER THREE

Gioachino Rossini

(1792-1868)

Rossini devoured his first thirty-two years like a starved mountain lion. During that period, he composed thirty-nine operas, all in record time. Legend has it that it took him eighteen days (or was it thirteen—or nineteen?) to compose *Il barbiere di Siviglia* (1816).

Rossini suffered a poor childhood. His father was a horn-player and his beautiful mother was an uneducated but accomplished singer of minor operatic parts. Rossini inherited his mother's looks and she protected him fiercely. When her brother-in-law insisted that with a small operation the young Gioacchino could bring in a lot of money as a castrato, his mother adamantly refused.

At the age of twelve, Rossini had composed six sonatas for two violins, cello and double bass. By the age of fifteen, he could play the violin and the harpsichord. By the age of twenty, he had penned six operas. Soon he became a celebrity—thanks to his popular operas, his dashing demeanor, his bons mots, and his beautiful voice.

When composing *Il barbiere di Seviglia*, he borrowed from himself. (For example, the overture was stolen from his own *Elisabetta d'Inghilterra*.) Opening night was a catastrophe. Geltrude Righetti-Giorgi, as Rosina, received boos as soon as she appeared. A stray cat ended up on the stage and Luigi Zamboni—who sang Figaro—tried to chase it away, earning "catcalls" from the audience. Another singer slipped and fell on a loose floorboard. Rossini himself at the keyboard was accused of applauding himself. He looked foolish in a ridiculous outfit (a saffron jacket with gold buttons) and furthermore, his enemies (those from an old school that opposed him) sneered and jeered. The audience was so boisterous that it was almost impossible to hear the first act.

Downcast, Rossini shut himself in his lodgings on the second night and promptly fell asleep. Suddenly, his impresario burst in the room, insisting he rush to the theater as there had been a standing ovation and the public was in ecstacy and wanted to thank him. "F—k the public!" Rossini said. Privately he revealed that he had lost faith in the public forever.

In 1822, Rossini met Ludwig van Beethoven (deaf and fading fast), who told the young musician: "Ah, Rossini. So you're the composer of *Il barbiere di Siviglia*. I congratulate you. It will be played as long as Italian opera exists. Never try to do anything else but **opera buffa**; any other style would do violence to your nature."

On crossing the Channel in 1823, Rossini suffered a horrible series of panic attacks and, once in London, he was incapacitated for days. His psychological problems eventually brought an end to his composing. Bloated and melancholy, he fell victim to a depression that completely debilitated him for much of his last forty years. Strangely enough, he outlived Bellini and Donizetti, his fellow **bel canto** composers. (**Bel canto**—or "beautiful singing"—was a style of opera in which the loveliness of the voice trumped both the words and the story.) Verdi was the last Italian composer left to speak to the new Romantic age.

Rossini died in Paris, not long after he had a meeting with the young Richard Wagner. "I must declare this," Wagner said as he left the apartment, "Of all the musicians I have met in Paris, he alone is truly great."

Il barbiere di Siviglia (1816)

This first aria was taken from Rossini's earlier flop, Aureliano in Palmira. In this scene, Count Almaviva sings a serenade for Rosina—the rich and beautiful ward of Dr. Bartolo.

Ecco Ridente (Almaviva, Act I)

Ecco ridente in cielo
Behold, smiling in the sky

spunta la bella aurora,
the lovely dawn is breaking,

e tu non sorgi ancora,
and you do not yet arise,

e puoi dormir così?
and you can sleep on like this?

Sorgi, mia dolce speme,
Arise, my sweet hope,

vieni, bell'idol mio,
come, my lovely adored one,

rendi men crudo, oh Dio!
Make less painful, oh Lord!

lo stral che me ferì.
the arrow that pierced me.

Oh sorte! già veggo
Oh fate! I already see

quel caro sembiante;
that dear face;

quest'anima amante
this loving soul

ottenne pietà.
has obtained mercy.

Oh istante d'amore!
Oh, moment of love!

Felice momento!
Happy moment!

Oh dolce contento!
Oh, sweet contentment!

che eguale non ha!
that has no equal!

VOCABULARY
la sorte: fate, destiny
Sono felice di tentare la sorte: I'm happy to tempt fate

già: already
te l'ho già detto: I have already told you
ma non ci conosciamo già? Haven't we met before?

l'anima: soul
con tutta l'anima: with all one's heart
vendere l'anima (al diavolo): to sell one's soul (to the devil)
anima gemella: soul mate
l'anima della festa: the life of the party

l'istante: moment, instant

in un istante: in a flash

fra un istante: in a moment

felice: happy

sono felice di fare la sua conoscenza: pleased to meet you (formal)

adesso sono più felice: I'm happier now

È stato il giorno più felice della mia vita: It was the happiest day of my life

eguale: equal

Loro sono ladri di eguale natura: They are thieves of equal nature.

Largo al factotum (Figaro, Act I)

Doesn't everyone know this aria? ("Figaro, Figaro, Figaro, Figaro!")

La ran la le ra,
La ran la le ra,

la ran la la.
la ran la la.

Largo al factotum
Make way for the jack-of-all-trades

della città.
of the city.

Presto, a bottega,
Quick, to the shop,

chè l'alba è già!
for it's already dawn!

Ah, che bel vivere,
Ah, what a lovely life,

che bel piacere,
what great good times,

per un barbiere
for a barber

di qualità!
of quality!

Ah bravo Figaro!
Ah! gallant Figaro!

Bravo, bravissimo!
Bravo, bravissimo!

Fortunatissimo,
A most fortunate man

per verità!
indeed!

Pronto a far tutto
Ready to do anything

la notte e il giorno,
by night and by day,

sempre d'intorno,
always present,

in giro sta.
he makes the rounds.

Miglior cuccagna
Greater good fortune

per un barbiere,
for a barber,

vita più nobile
a more illustrious life

no, non si dà.
doesn't exist, no.

Rasori e pettini,
Razors and combs,

lancette e forbici,
lancets and scisssors

al mio commando
my orders

tutto qui sta.
all await.

V'è la risorsa
Then, there are the resources

poi del mio mestiere
of my profession

con la donnetta,
with the ladies,

col cavaliere…(etc.)
with the gentlemen…(etc.)

Ah che bel vivere,
Ah, what a lovely life,

che bel piacere
what great good times

per un barbiere
for a barber

di qualità!
of quality!

Tutti mi chiedono
Everyone asks for me,

tutti mi vogliono:
everybody wants me:

donne, ragazzi,
ladies, boys,

vecchi, fanciulle.
old men, girls.

Qua la parrucca…
The wig over here…

Presto la barba!
Quick, a shave!

Qua la sanguigna…
A bloodletting over here…

Presto, il biglietto!
Quick, a message!

Figaro! Figaro!

Ahimè, che furia!
Alas, what a fury!

Ahimè, che follia!
Alas, what madness!

Uno alla volta,
One at a time,

per carita! (etc.)
for pity's sake!

Figaro…son qua!
Figaro…I'm here!

Ehi, Figaro! Son qua!
Hey, Figaro! I'm here!

Figaro qua…Figaro là…
Figaro here…Figaro there…

Figaro su…Figaro giù
Figaro up…Figaro down

Pronto, prontissimo!
I'm coming, I'm coming right away!

Son come il fulmine!
I'm like lightening!

Sono il factotum
I'm the jack-of-all-trades

della città!
of the city!

Ah, bravo Figaro!
Ah, gallant Figaro!

Bravo, bravissimo! (etc.)
Bravo, bravissimo!

A te fortuna non mancherà! (etc.)
You will never want for good luck!

VOCABULARY

il barbiere: barber
fa il barbiere: he's a barber
devo andare dal barbiere: I need a haircut.

la barba: beard
ha la barba: he's got a beard
farsi la barba: to shave
mi faccio la barba: I shave
si fa la barba: he shaves
ma mi sono fatto crescere la barba per te! But (honey), I grew facial hair for you!
che barba! What a bore!

la bottega: shop
le botteghe: shops

l'alba: dawn
all'alba: at dawn, at daybreak
alzarsi all'alba: to get up at dawn
spunta l'alba: dawn is breaking

vivere: to live
vivere fino a 100 anni: to live to be 100
vivi e lascia vivere: live and let live
viviamo insieme: we live together
ho giusto di che vivere: I have just enough to live on

fortunato: lucky, fortunate
sei più fortunato di me: you're luckier than I am
numero fortunato: lucky number

la verità: truth
hai detto la verità? Did you tell the truth?

macchina dell verità: lie-detector
la verità nuda e cruda: the plain unvarnished truth

il giro: turn
andare in giro: to wander about, walk around
giro turistico della città: sightseeing tour of the city

la cuccagna: abundance, plenty
paese della cuccagna: land of plenty
È finita la cuccagna! The party's over!

il mestiere: job, trade, skill
di mestiere: by trade
un mestiere difficile: a difficult job
Cosa fai di mestiere? What do you do?
fa il mestiere di calzolaio: he is a shoemaker
imparare un mestiere: to learn a trade

la parrucca: wig
le parruche: wigs
Indossavo una nuova parrucca: I was wearing a new wig.

ahimè: alas

la follia: madness
in un momento di follia: in a moment of madness
lo amo alla follia: I'm madly in love with him
È una follia! It's crazy!

la volta: time
una volta: once
una volta alla settimana: once a week
certe volte sono un po' triste: I feel a bit down sometimes.
ogni volta: every time

CHAPTER FOUR

Gaetano Donizetti

(1797-1848)

As if in a race against time, Donizetti composed seventy operas by the age of fifty-one. *Lucia di Lammermoor* (1835)—based on Sir Walter Scott's novel *The Bride of Lammermoor* (1819)—is the most performed of his serious operas. He wrote for the general public, getting them to tap their feet to the wonderful melodies he created.

Rossini had retired and Vincenzo Bellini had died by the time *Lucia* premiered, making Donizetti the most important composer of Italian opera.

Unfortunately, in 1845 he was diagnosed with cerebro-spinal syphilis and severe mental illness. He was forced to enter a mental institution by early 1846. A year later, his friends moved him back to his native town of Bergamo, where he died in April 1848. An unhappy end for the man who had written the greatest mad scene in all of opera.

Lucia di Lammermoor is a **dramma tragico** (tragic opera) set in the atmospheric, fog-caked hills of Scotland. The character of Lucia—who goes from ecstasy to insanity in three acts—provides for a demanding role. Two notable sopranos of the bel canto revival in the 1950's—Maria Callas and Dame Joan Sutherland—approached the challenge differently. Callas sang the opera **come scritto** (as written), while Sutherland used her coloratura skills to tickle her vocal chords into a frenzy as unhinged as Lucia's mindset.

Lucia di Lammermoor (1835)

A **dramma tragico** about warring families, in which Lucia is barred from marrying her true love, Edgardo, by her brother Enrico who wants her to make a politically (and financially) advantageous match. In short, she is forced to marry Arturo, and on her wedding night she loses her mind and stabs him to death. Who can forget the famous blood-splattered nightgown she appears in during the "mad scene"?

Regnava nel silenzio (Lucia, Act I)

Here, Lucia is with her companion Alisa, staring into a fountain and recalling that it holds the corpse of an ancestor murdered by a jealous lover. She describes the vision of the ghost as it appeared to her.

Regnava nel silenzio
Silence reigned.

alta la notte e bruna,
It was late and the night was dark.

colpìa la fonte un pallido
shining in the fountain was a pale

raggio di tetra luna,
ray of moonlight

quando sommesso un gemito
Suddenly I heard a stifled cry

fra l'aure udir sì fe',
that seemed to float on the breeze

ed ecco su quel margine,
And there on the fountain's edge

l'ombra mostrarsi a me!
her ghost showed itself to me!

Qual di chi parla muoversi
She who spoke moved

il labbro suo vedea,
her lip I saw

e con la mano esanime
and with the lifeless hand

chiamarmi a sè parea;
she seemed to call me to her

stette un momento immobile,
motionless for a moment,

poi ratta, dileguò,
And then she vanished.

e l'onda pria sì limpida,
And the water, which had been so clear,

di sangue rosseggiò
became red with blood!

VOCABULARY

la fonte: spring, source

il raggio: ray, beam
un raggio di sole: a ray of sunshine
un raggio di speranza: gleam of hope

ecco: here

ecco i nostri amici: here are our friends

ecco il treno: here's the train

eccomi: here I am

parla: he/she speaks

parlare: to talk, to speak

il bambino non sa ancora parlare: the baby can't talk yet

parla bene! Talk properly!

il labbro: lip

le labbra: lips

chiamarmi: to call me

chiamare: to call, phone

hanno chiamato la polizia: they called the police

poi: then, later on, at last

prima o poi: sooner or later

a poi: till later

l'onda: wave

limpido, a: clear, lucid

il cielo è limpido e blu: the sky is clear and blue.

il sangue: blood

uccidere a sangue freddo: to kill in cold blood

ha la musica nel sangue: music is in his blood

Quando rapito in estasi (Lucia, Act I)

In happier days, as she is about to meet Edgardo…

Quando rapito in estasi
When I am caught in the rapture

del più cocente ardore,
of his burning love.

col favellar del core,
With the speech of his heart

mi giura eterna fè.
he swears me eternal faith.

Gli affanni miei dimentico,
All of my troubles I forget,

gioia diviene il pianto,
my sorrow turns to joy.

parmi che a lui d'accanto
When he is near to me

si schiuda il ciel per me!
it is as if heaven opened to me!

VOCABULARY

giura: he/she swears
giurare: to swear
È vero, te lo giuro! It's true, I swear!

gli affanni: sorrows

dimentico: I forget
dimenticare: to forget
Ho dimenticato il tuo numero di telefono: I've forgotten your phone number

accanto: nearby, near, next to, beside
abito qui accanto: I live next door
Siediti accanto a me: Sit next to me

Il dolce suono (Lucia, Act II)

The famous mad scene…

> **Il dolce suono**
> The sweet sound
>
> **mi colpì di sua voce!**
> of his voice has struck me!
>
> **Ah! quella voce!**
> Ah! That voice!
>
> **m'è qui nel cor discesa!**
> has entered my heart here!
>
> **Edgardo! io ti son resa;**
> Edgardo! I am restored to you;
>
> **fuggita io son da' tuoi nemici.**
> I've escaped from your enemies.
>
> **Un gelo mi serpeggia nel sen!**
> A chill crawls through my chest!

Trema ogni fibra! Vacilla il piè!
Every nerve quivers! My feet totter!

Presso la fronte meco t'assidi alquanto,
Sit with me by the fountain for a while,

sì, presso la fonte meco t'assidi!
yes, sit with me buy the fountain!

Ohimè! sorge il tremendo fantasma
Alas! The fearful ghost rises up

e ne separa!
and separates us!
Ahimè, ahimè, Edgardo!
Alas! Alas! Edgardo!

Edgardo! ah! il fantasma ne separa!
Edgardo! Ah! The ghost separates us!

Qui ricovriamo, Edgardo,
Let's seek refuge here, Edgardo,

a piè dell'ara.
at the foot of the altar.

Sparsa è di rose!
It's strewn with roses!

Un'armonia celeste,
Heavenly music,

di', non ascolti?
Tell me, don't you hear it?

Ah! l'inno suona di nozze!
Ah! the wedding hymn sounds!

Ah, l'inno di nozze!
Ah, the wedding hymn!

Il rito per noi s'appresta.
They're preparing the ceremony for us!

Oh me felice!
Oh, how happy I am!

Oh gioia che si sente, e non si dice!
Oh! Joy that is felt and can't be expressed!

Ardon gl'incensi—
The incense burns—

Splendon le sacre faci intorno!
The holy lights shine all around!

Ecco il ministro!
Here is the pastor!

Porgimi la destra!
Give me your right hand!

Oh lieto giorno!
Oh joyous day!

Oh lieto!
Oh joyous!

Alfin son tua, alfin sei mio,
At last I'm yours, at last you're mine,

a me ti dona un Dio.
God bestows you on me.

[dialogue for Normanno, Raimondo and Chorus]
Ogni piacer più grato,
All the greatest delights,

sì, ogni piacere mi fia con te diviso—
yes, all delights I shall share with you—

Del ciel clemente un riso
a smile from merciful heaven.

[dialogue for Raimondo, Enrico and Chorus]
Che chiedi?
What are you asking for?

Ah, me misera!
Ah! Wretched me!

Non mi guardar sì fiero,
Don't look at me so fiercely,

segnai quel foglio, è vero, sì, è vero.
I signed that paper, it's true, yes, it's true.

Nell'ira sua terribile
In his awful rage

calpesta, oh Dio, l'anello!
he stamps on the ring, oh God!

Mi maledice!
He curses me!

Ah! vittima fui d'un crudel fratello:
Ah! I was the victim of a cruel brother:

ma ognor, ognor t'amai,
but I always, always loved you,

ognor, Edgardo,
always, Edgardo,

sì, ognor, ognor t'amai
yes, I always, always loved you

[dialogue for Enrico and Raimondo]
ah! e t'amo ancor!
ah! and I love you still!

Edgardo mio, sì, te lo guiro!
Yes, my Edgardo, I swear it to you!

Chi mi nomasti? Arturo!
Whom did you speak to me of? Arturo!

Tu nomasti, Arturo!
You spoke of Arturo!

Ah! non fuggir! Ah, per pietà!
Ah! Don't run away! Ah, for pity's sake!

No, non fuggir! ah perdon!
No, don't run away! Ah forgive me!

[dialogue for Enrico, Raimondo and Chorus]
Ah! no, non fuggir, Edgardo!
Ah, no, don't run away, Edgardo!

Spargi d'amaro pianto,
Shed bitter tears

il mio terrestre velo,
on my earthly shroud,

mentre lassù nel cielo,
while up there in heaven,

io pregherò per te.
I'll pray for you.

Al giunger tuo soltanto
Only when you arrive

fia bello il ciel per me!
will heaven be beautiful for me!

[dialogue for Enrico, Raimondo, and Chorus]
Spargi (etc.)...per me!
Shed (etc.)...for me!

Ah! ch'io spiri accanto a te,
Ah! That I might die beside you,

appresso a te!
close to you!

VOCABULARY
il suono: sound
ballare al suono di un'orchestra: to dance to the music of an orchestra

la voce: voice
ho perso la voce: I've lost my voice
la voce della coscienza: the voice of conscience
parlare a alta voce: to speak loudly
parlare a bassa voce: to speak quietly

il nemico: enemy
ha molti nemici: he has a lot of enemies
territorio nemico: enemy territory

simpatico: nice, pleasant, likeable
antipatico: unpleasant, disagreeable

sparso, a: scattered
ho sparso le sue ceneri: I scattered his ashes

ascolti: (you) listen
ascoltare: to listen to
Mi stai ascoltando? Are you listening to me?
ascoltare la messa: to attend Mass

le nozze: wedding, marriage
regalo di nozze: wedding present
viaggio di nozze: honeymoon
Dove andate in viaggio di nozze? Where are you going on your
   honeymoon?

clemente: merciful, mild

chiedi: you ask
chiedere: to ask
mi ha chiesto l'ora: he asked me the time
Chiedi a Lidia come si chiama il suo cane: Ask Lidia what her dog's
   name is.

misero, a: miserable, wretched, pitiful
fare una misera figura: to cut a poor figure
una misera scusa: a lame excuse

non fuggire: don't run away
fuggire: to avoid, shun, run away, flee
È fuggito di prigione: he escaped from jail

CHAPTER FIVE

Vincenzo Bellini

(1801-1835)

Bellini only lived for thirty-four years, but in that short time he made his mark on the music world with his nine operas. He was born in Sicily, where his father played the organ and was a respected composer. There is spotty evidence to show what a child prodigy he was ("he started studying music theory at the age of two and the piano at three, etc."), as it is always fashionable to be an early bloomer. At the age of fifteen, he studied music and composed under the tutelage of his grandfather. Three years later, he gained entrance to a fancy conservatory in Naples (Conservatorio di San Sebastiano), where he studied with boys a little younger than he from 5:15 am to 10 pm each day. The emphasis was more on Haydn and Mozart than Rossini.

The artistic director of the school was Niccolò Antonio Zingarelli and he gave Bellini this advice: "If your compositions 'sing,' your music will most certainly please...Therefore, if you train your heart to give you melody and then you set it forth as simply as possible, your success will be assured. You will become a composer. Otherwise, you will end up being a good organist in some village."

Love for a young woman whom he tutored spurred on the composition of his first opera in 1824—*Adelson e Salvini*. However, his three greatest works—*La Sonnambula* (1831), *Norma* (1831) and *I Puritani* (1835)—came several years later.

I'm focusing here on *Norma*—an opera about a high priestess of the Druid temple. *Norma* premiered at La Scala, but it took a while for it to grow on audiences. Bellini revised his "Casta diva" ("Chaste Goddess") aria eight times before he was satisfied with it. Bathed in moonlight, Norma is to cut the sacred mistletoe to mark the beginning of the Druid uprising against Roman occupation. She declares the time for military action is not ripe. Norma then prays to the moon goddess for guidance.

Norma (1831)
Casta diva (Norma, Act I)

Io nei volumi arcani
I am reading the arcane volumes

leggo del cielo;
of the sky;

in pagine di morte della superba Roma
on pages of death the name of haughty Rome

è scritto il nome—
is inscribed—

Ella un giorno morrà;
One day she will die;

ma non per voi
but not by your hands.

Morrà pei vizi suoi,
She will die of her own vices,

qual consunta morrà.
Like a ravaged woman she will die

L'ora aspettate,
Await the hour,

l'ora fatal che compia il gran discreto.
the fatal hour that fulfills the grand decree.

Pace v'intimo—e il sacro vischio io mieto.
I bid you peace—and I will pick the sacred mistletoe.

Casta diva, che inargenti
Chaste goddess who silvers

queste sacre antiche piante,
these sacred ancient trees,

a noi volgi il bel sembiante
turn your lovely face toward us,

senza nube e senza vel.
cloudless and unveiled.

[Orovesco and Chorus: Casta (etc.)]

Tempra tu de'cori ardenti,
Temper our ardent hearts,

tempra ancor lo zelo audace,
continue to temper the bold zeal

spargi in terra quella pace
spread over earth that peace

che regnar tu fai nel ciel.
which you cause to reign in heaven.

Fine al rito; e il sacro bosco
End the ritual; and let the sacred wood

sia disgombro dai profani.
be cleared of the holy ones.

Quando il Nume irato e fosco
When the wrathful and dark deity

chiegga il sangue dei Romani,
demands the blood of the Romans,

dal Druïdico delubro
from the Druids' temple

la mia voce tuonerà.
my voice shall resound.

[Chorus: **Tuoni, e un sol del popol empio**
[Chorus: Let it resound and of the impious nation

non isfugga al giusto scempio,
let not one escape his just slaughter,

e premier da noi percosso
and, the first to be struck by us,

il Proconsole cadrà.]
the Proconsul shall fall.]

Sì, cadrà—punirlo io posso—
Yes, he will fall—I can punish him—

(Ma punirlo il cor non sa.)
(But my heart knows not how to punish him.)

(Ah! Bello a me ritorna
(Ah! Come back to me in the beauty

del fido amor primiero;
of your first true love;

e contro il mondo intero
and against the whole world

difesa a te sarò.
I shall be your protection.

Ah! Bello a me ritorna
Ah! Come back to me in the beauty

del raggio tuo sereno;
of your tranquil radiance;

e vita nel tuo seno,
and life in your breast,

e patria, e cielo avrò.)
and homeland and heaven I shall find.)

[Chorus: Sei lento, sì, sei lento,
[Chorus: You are slow, yes, you are slow,

o giorno di vendetta;
o day of vengeance;

ma irato il Dio t'affretta
but you are hastened by the angry god

che il Tebro condannò.]
who has condemned the Tiber.]

(Ah! riedi ancora
(Ah! return again

qual eri allora,
as you were then,

quando il cor ti diedi! etc.)
when I gave you my heart! etc.)

VOCABULARY

leggo: I read

leggere: to read

leggere ad alta voce: to read aloud

leggere fra le righe: to read between the lines

Present tense conjugation of leggere:	
(io) leggo	I read
(tu) leggi	you (singular) read
(lui, lei, Lei) legge	he, she, you (formal) reads
(noi) leggiamo	we read
(voi) leggete	you (plural) read
(loro) leggono	they read

le pagine: pages

superba: haughty, proud

è scritto: it is written

scrivere: to write

come si scrive questa parola? How do you write/spell this word?

casto, a: chaste, pure

diva: goddess

senza nube: without clouds

ancora: even, more, still

tu fai: you do

fare: to make, to do

fare un errore: to make a mistake

fare una festa: to hold a party

hai fatto il letto? Have you made the bed?

irato: irate, furious

tuonerà: it will thunder, boom

tuo seno: your breast
il seno: bosom, breast, womb
portare un figlio in seno: to carry a child in one's womb
in seno alla famiglia: in the bosom of the family

la patria: homeland, fatherland
Vienna, la patria del walzer: Vienna, the home of the waltz
tornare in patria: to return to one's own country
amor di patria: patriotism

t'affretta: hasten you

CHAPTER SIX

Giuseppe Verdi
(1813-1901)

When little Giuseppe was eight years old, his father (a taverner) bought him a spinet (an upright harpsichord). He grew into a serious adolescent. At nineteen, he applied to the Milan Conservatory and was rejected for his advanced age and his status as a "foreigner." (He was from the province of Parma.)

At twenty-three, he was named to lead secular music in Busseto—the town next to his native Le Roncole. That same year, he got married to Margherita Barezzi. They quickly had two children. Both children died, followed by their mother in 1840. Verdi's opera—*Un giorno di regno*—flopped that same year. Verdi wanted to throw in the towel.

Then he opened a libretto at random and found the page with the lines "Va, pensiero, sull'ali dorati" ("Go, thought, on golden wings"). Soon he had his first hit—*Nabucco* (1842)—and the "golden wings" chorus that evoked the Hebrew slaves' lament for their fatherland hit a chord for many Italians living under Austrian rule.

Several years later, Italians would associate Verdi with the Risorgimento (the revolutionary movement for Italian liberation and unification). In fact, "Viva Verdi!" was shouted in the streets as a political slogan that signified "**Viva V**ittorio **E**manuele **Re D'I**talia" ("Long live Victor Emmanuel, King of Italy").

Verdi composed the entire score for *Rigoletto* (1851) in forty days. Here we have the lustful Duke of Mantua disguised as a student so that he may seduce Gilda, without realizing that she is the daughter of his jester Rigoletto. Rigoletto helps the courtiers abduct a woman, without knowing that it is his daughter Gilda. Rigoletto learns that the Duke has bedded her and he hires an assassin, Sparafucile. Sparafucile has a sister named Maddalena who has caught the Duke's attention and she begs for the Duke's life. Sparafucile vows to kill the next person who walks through the door. It is Gilda. Early in the opera, Count Monterone (whose daughter has been "ruined" by the Duke) curses Rigoletto. **La maledizione** (the curse) has taken effect.

Rigoletto (1851)

Here the Duke is assessing his future conquests…

Questa o quella (Duke, Act I)

Questo o quella per me pari sono
To me this woman or that one are the same as

a quant'altre d'intorno mi vedo;
all the others I see around me;

del mio core l'impero non cedo,
I don't surrender command of my heart

meglio ad una che ad altra beltà.
to one beauty any more than to another.

La costoro avvenenza è qual dono,
Their comeliness is like a gift

di che il fato ne infiora la vita;
with which fortune decorates our life.

s'oggi questa mi torna gradita
If this one finds favor with me today,

forse un altra doman lo sarà.
tomorrow perhaps it will be another.

La costanza, tiranna del core,
Fidelity, despot of the heart,

detestiamo qual morbo crudele;
we hate like a true plague;

sol chi vuole si serbi fedele.
Let only those remain faithful who wish to.

Non v'ha amor se non v'è libertà.
There's no love where there's no liberty.

De' martiri il geloso furore,
I scorn the jealous rage of husbands,

degli amanti le smanie deride;
and the frenzy of lovers;

anco d'Argo i cent'occhi disfido,
I defy even Argus' hundred eyes

se mi punge una qualche beltà.
If some beauty allures me.

VOCABULARY

intorno: around

qui/lì intorno: around here/there

erano seduti intorno al tavolo: they were sitting around the table

oggi: today

domani: tomorrow

ieri: yesterday

fedele: faithful

essere fedele a: to be faithful to

un marito fedele: a faithful husband

infedele: unfaithful

Pari siamo (Rigoletto, Act II)

Rigoletto thinks about Count Monterone's curse...

Pari siamo! Io la lingua, egli ha il pugnale;
We're equals! I have my tongue, he has his dagger.

l'uomo son io che ride, ei quel che spegne!
I'm the man who mocks, he the one who murders!

Quel vecchio maledivami!
That old man cursed me!

O uomini!—o natura!—
O mankind!—O nature!—

vil schelerato mi faceste voi!
You made me a wicked wretch!

Oh rabbia! esser diforme! esser buffone!
Oh fury! To be deformed! To be a jester!

Non dover, non poter altro che ridere!
Not to be permitted, not to be able to do other than joke!

Il retaggio d'ogni uom m'è tolto, il pianto!
Every man's legacy is forbidden to me: weeping!

Questo padrone mio
This master of mine

giovin, giocondo, sì possente, bello, sonnechhiando mi dice:
youthful, gay, so powerful, handsome, as he dozes off tells me:

Fa ch'io rida, buffone...
"Make me laugh, clown..."

forzarmi deggio e farlo!
And I must force myself to do it!

Oh dannazione!
Oh, damnation!

Odio a voi, cortegiani schernitori!
I hate you, jeering courtiers!

Quanta in mordervi ho gioia!
How much I enjoy needling you!

Se inquio son, per cagion vostra è solo.
If I'm wicked, it's only because of you.

Ma in altr'uomo qui mi cangio!
But here I transform myself into another man!

Quel vecchio maledivami...Tal pensiero
That old man cursed me...Why is that thought

perchè conturba ognor la mente mia?
constantly disturbing my mind?

Mi coglierà sventura? Ah no, è follia!
Will misfortune befall me? Ah, no, that's madness!

VOCABULARY

pari siamo: we're equals
pari: equal, (the) same
hanno pari diritti: they have equal rights

la lingua: tongue
mostro la lingua a Luigi: I stick my tongue out at Luigi
non parliamo la stessa lingua: we don't speak the same language
la rabbia: anger, rage
farsi prendere della rabbia: to fly into a rage
Che rabbia! What a damned nuisance!

il buffone: clown, buffoon
fare il buffone: to clown around

il padrone: master, owner, boss
la padrona: mistress, owner, boss
chi è padrone di questo gatto? Who's the owner of this cat?
Sono il padrone della bottega: I am the owner of this store.

inquio, a: iniquitous
inquinare: to pollute
Le fabbriche non hanno il diritto di inquinare il mare: The factories don't have the right to pollute the sea

la sventura: misfortune
Questa è la sventura della nostra famiglia: This is the misfortune of our family.

Caro nome (Gilda, Act II)

Gilda falsely believes that the Duke is a student named Gualtier Maldè…

Gualtier Maldè! nome di lui sì amato!
Gualtier Maldè! name of him so beloved,

ti scolpisci nel core innamorato!
you are engraved in my adoring heart!

Caro nome che il mio cor
Precious name, the first

festi primo palpitar,
that caused my heart to throb,

le delizie dell'amor
of love's delights

mi dei sempre rammentar!
you'll remind me always!

Col pensiero il mio desir
Along with my thoughts my longing

A te sempre volerà,
will ever fly to you,

e fin l'ultimo sospir,
and until my dying breath,

caro nome, tuo sarà.
precious name, they'll be of you.

VOCABULARY

innamorato, a (di): in love (with)

Sei innamorata di lui? Are you in love with him?

È innamorato perso: He's madly in love.

le delizie: delights, treats, delicacies

delizie del lontano Est: delicacies of the Far East

ultimo, a: last, final, latest

arrivare per ultimo: to arrive last

Gianni è arrivato per ultimo alla festa: Gianni arrived last at the party.

l'ultima volta che l'ho visto: the last time I saw him

Hai visto l'ultimo film di Nanni Moretti? Have you seen Nanni Moretti's latest film?

Parmi veder le lagrime (Duke, Act III)

The Duke returns to Rigoletto's house and finds Gilda gone…

> **Ella mi fu rapita!**
> She was stolen from me!

> **E quando, o ciel? ne' brevi istanti,**
> And when, o heavens? In the brief moments

> **prima che il mio presagio interno**
> before my inner foreboding

> **sull'orma corsa ancora mi spingesse!**
> urged me back over the route I had taken!

> **Schiuso era l'uscio! e la magion deserta!**
> The door was open! And the house empty!

E dove ora sarà quell' angiol caro?
And where is that precious angel now?

Colei che prima potè in questo core
She was the first who could in this heart

destar la fiamma di costanti affetti?
could light the flame of steadfast love?

Colei sì pura, al cui modesto sguardo
She so pure, at whose modest glance

quasi spinto a virtù talor mi credo!
I almost believe myself at times inclined towards virtue!

Ella mi fu rapita!
She was stolen from me!

E chi l'ardiva?—me ne andrò vendetta:
And who dared to do it?—but I'll be avenged!

Lo chiede il pianto della mia diletta.
The tears of my beloved demand it!

Parmi veder le lagrime
I seem to see the tears

scorrenti da quel ciglio,
flowing from those lashes,

quando fra il dubbio e l'ansia
when, between her worry and fear

del subito periglio,
of impending danger,

dell'amor nostro memore
mindful of our love

il suo Gualtier chiamò.
she called for her Gualtier.

Ned ei potea soccorerti,
And he could not help you,

cara fanciulla amata;
dear beloved maid;

ei che vorria coll'anima
he that with all his soul would

farti quaggiù beata;
give you bliss in this world;

ei che le sfere agl'angeli
that the angels for their heavenly spheres

per te non invidiò!
because of you he did not envy!

VOCABULARY

l'uscio: door
sull'uscio: on the doorstep

la porta: door, doorstep, doorway, gate, goal, port
chiudi la porta, per cortesia: close the door, please
vendere porta a porta: to sell from door to door
lo hanno messo alla porta: they kicked him out
porta USB: USB port

la fiamma: flame
una vecchia fiamma: an old flame
le fiamme dell'inferno: hellfire

rapito, a: kidnapped
un rapito, una rapita: a kidnapped person
rapire: to kidnap, abduct

il periglio: peril

la fanciulla: girl, maiden
Andiamo a cercare la nostra fanciulla: We're going in search of our
  maiden.

Cortigiani (Rigoletto, Act III)

Rigoletto tries to save his daughter Gilda…

> **Cortigiani, vil razza dannata,**
> Courtiers, you damned vile race,
>
> **per qual prezzo vendeste il mio bene?**
> for how much did you sell my darling?
>
> **A voi nulla per l'oro sconviene!**
> There's nothing you wouldn't do for gold!
>
> **Ma mia figlia è impagabil tesor.**
> But my daughter is a priceless treasure.
>
> **La rendete…o, se pur disarmata,**
> Give her back…or even without weapons,
>
> **questa man per voi fora cruente;**
> this hand will be stained with your blood;

nulla in terra più l'uomo paventa,
a man fears nothing more on earth

se dei figli difende l'onor.
when defending his children's honor.

Quella porta, assassin, m'aprite!
Open that door for me, murderers!

Ah! voi tutti a me contro venite!
Ah! You're all against me!

Ebben—piango...Marullo—signore,
Well then—I'll weep...Marullo—sir,

tu ch'hai l'alma gentil come il core,
you whose soul is kind like your heart,

dimmi or tu, dove l'hanno nascosta?
you tell me, where have they hidden her?

È là? Non è vero? Tu taci! Ohimè!
She's there? Isn't it so? You keep silent! Oh, woe!

Miei signori, perdono, pietate—
My lords, pardon, have pùity—

al vegliardo la figlia ridate.
return an old man's daughter to him!

Il ridarla a voi nulla ora costa,
It will cost you nothing to return her now,

tutto al mondo è tal figlia per me.
that daughter is all the world to me.

VOCABULARY

il prezzo: price
a buon prezzo: cheaply, at a good price
menù a prezzo fisso: set-price menu
tirare sul prezzo: to bargain, haggle
un prezzo ragionevole: a reasonable price

la terra: earth
sulla faccia della terra: on the face of the earth
la terra è bagnata: the ground is wet
la mia terra: my native land
la Terra Santa: The Holy Land

nascosto, a: hidden
nascondere: to hide, conceal
nascondere il viso fra le mani: to bury one's face in one's hands
Non ho qualcosa da nascondere: I don't have anything to hide

La donna è mobile (Duke, Act IV)

The Duke sings of the inconstant nature of women…

La donna è mobile
Woman is fickle

qual piuma al vento,
as a feather in the breeze,

muta d'accento
she changes her words

e di pensiero.
and her thoughts.

Sempre un'amabile,
Ever a lovable,

leggiadro viso,
graceful countenance,

in pianto o in riso,
weeping or smiling,

è menzognero.
it's deceitful.

È sempre misero
That man is always wretched

chi a lei s'affida,
who places faith in her,

chi le confida
who entrusts to her

mal cauto il core!
his heart misguidedly!

Pur mai non sentesi
Yet that man never feels

felice appieno,
thoroughly happy,

chi su quel seno
who on that bosom

non liba amore!
doesn't taste love!

VOCABULARY

mobile: moving, mobile
un mobile: a piece of furniture
un negozio di mobili: a furniture shop

la piuma: feather
guanciale di piume: feather pillow
leggero come una piuma: light as a feather

il vento: wind
c'è vento: it's windy
contro vento: against the wind
parlare al vento: to waste one's breath

menzognero, a : false, untrue, lying

Aïda (1871)

Rademes—captain of the Egyptian guard—dreams of winning the beautiful Aïda—an Ethiopian princess...

Celeste Aïda (Radames, Act I)

Se quel guerrier io fossi!
If only I were that warrior!

Se il mio sogno si avverasse!
If my dream came true!

Un esercito di prodi da me guidato,
An army of brave men led by me,

e la vittoria, e il plauso di Menfi tutta!
and victory, and the plaudits of all of Memphis!

e a te, mia dolce Aïda,
and to return to you, my sweet Aïda,

tornar di lauri cinto…
wreathed in laurels…

dirti, "Per te ho pugnato, per te ho vinto!"
to say to you, "I fought for your sake, I conquered for your sake!"

Celeste Aïda, forma divina,
Heavenly Aïda, divine form,

mistico serto di luce e fior,
mystic garland of light and blossom,

del mio pensiero tu sei regina,
you are the queen of my thoughts,

tu di mia vita sei lo splendor.
You are the glory of my life.

Il tuo bel cielo vorrei ridarti,
I would like to restore to you your lovely sky,

le dolci brezze del patria suol;
the soft breezes of your native land;

un regal serto sul crin posarti,
to place a royal wreath on your locks,

ergerti un trono vicino al sol, ah!
to raise a throne for you beside the sun, ah!

Celeste Aïda, forma divina,
Heavenly Aïda, divine form,

mistico raggio di luce e fior,
mystic ray of light and blossom,

del mio pensiero tu sei regina (etc.)
you are the queen of my thoughts (etc.)

...sol!
...the sun!

VOCABULARY

il guerriero: warrior
la guerra: war
la prima guerra mondiale: World War I
la seconda guerra mondiale: World War II
guerra fredda: cold war

l'esercito: army
Sappiamo che state formando un esercito: We know you are forming an army.

la vittoria: victory

ho pugnato: I fought
pugnare: to fight

ho vinto: I won
vincere: to win
vincere un premio: to win a prize
ho vinto la paura: I got over my fear

la regina: queen
la regina Elisabetta: Queen Elizabeth
la regina della festa: the belle of the ball

il trono: throne
salire/ascendere al trono: to come to/to ascend the throne

CHAPTER SEVEN

Giacomo Puccini

(1858-1924)

I probably should have started with Puccini! The language of the librettos he used is simple and straightforward—a sure sign of the **verismo** movement he championed (**verismo** meaning "truth"—or the avoidance of everything in opera that ressembles "artistry" or "technique"). Puccini is often taken as a guilty pleasure because he's possibly the most popular opera composer. (No wonder William Berger titled his book *Puccini Without Excuses*.) Think of all the crowd-pleasers such as *Tosca* (1900) and *Madama Butterfly* (1904)! Here we will look at *La bohème* and *La fanciulla del West*.

La bohème (The Bohemians) is a story about real, ordinary people. (We are a long way from Handel's *Alcina* and the sorceress' enchanted island!) Rodolfo lives in a Parisian garret with three friends. It it Christmas Eve and they are cold and hungry. Suddenly, one of the roomates has a windfall and they all head out to celebrate, except for Rodolfo who wants to finish an article he's writing. There is a knock on the door. It's Mimì, a pretty, delicate young woman who lives in the apartment below. She asks him if he would light her candle. He does so, and as she is getting ready to leave, she drops her key and both of their candles are extinguished. They are fumbling in the dark...when Rodolfo sings **Che gelida manina**...

La bohème (1896)
Che gelida manina (Rodolfo, Act I)

Che gelida manina,
What an ice-cold little hand,

se la lasci riscaldar.
won't you let me warm it?

Cercar che giova?
What's the use of searching?

Al buio non si trova.
We won't find it [the lost key] in the dark.

Ma per fortuna
But luckily,

è una notte di luna
it's a moonlit night

e qui la luna
and up here the moon

l'abbiamo vicina.
we have it nearby.

Aspetti, signorina,
Wait, Miss,

le dirò con due parole
and I'll tell you in a couple of words

chi son, e che faccio,
who I am and what I do,

come vivo. Vuole?
how I live. Would you like that?

Chi son? Sono un poeta.
Who am I? I'm a poet.

Che cosa faccio? Scrivo.
What do I do? I write.

E come vivo? Vivo.
And how do I live? I live.

In povertà mia lieta
In my merry poverty

scialo da gran signore
like a great lord I squander

rime e inni d'amore.
poems and hymns of love.

Per sogni e per chimere
For dreams and fantasies

e per castelli in aria
and castles in the air

l'anima ho milionaria.
I have the soul of a millionaire.

Talor dal mio forziere
Occasionally from my strongbox

ruban tutti i gioielli
all the gems are stolen

due ladri: gli occhi belli.
by two thieves: beautiful eyes.

V'entrar con voi pur ora,
Just now they came in with you,

ed i miei sogni usati,
and worn-out dreams,

e i bei sogni miei
my lovely dreams,

tosto si dileguar!
quickly faded!

Ma il furto non m'accora
But the theft doesn't distress me

poichè v'ha preso stanza
because in its place

la [dolce] speranza!
there's such a [pleasant] hope!

Or che mi conoscete,
Now that you know me,

parlate voi, deh!
you speak, I beg you!

Parlate! Chi siete!
Speak! Who are you?

Vi piaccia dir!
Please tell me!

VOCABULARY

gelido, a: freezing, ice-cold
il gelato: ice cream
il gelo: intense cold, frost
sentirsi il gelo nelle ossa: to feel a chill of fear

la mano: hand
la manina: little hand

riscaldare: to heat, to warm
caldo, a: warm
fa caldo: it's warm

il buio: dark, darkness
al buio: in the dark
ho paura del buio: I'm afraid of the dark

per fortuna: fortunately

la luna: moon
il sole: sun

chi sono: who I am
che faccio: what I do
come vivo: how I live

il poeta: poet
scrivo: I write
scrivere: to write

la povertà: poverty

la rima: rhyme, verse
rima baciata: rhyming couplet
rima alternate: alternate rhymes

l'inno: hymn
inno nazionale: national anthem

il sogno: dream
un brutto sogno: a bad dream
ho fatto uno strano sogno: I had a strange dream

il furto: theft
vorrei denunciare un furto: I'd like to report a theft

Mi chiamano Mimì (Mimì, Act I)

Mimì answers with her own introduction…

> **Sì. Mi chiamano Mimì,**
> Yes. They call me Mimì,
>
> **ma il mio nome è Lucia.**
> but my name is Lucia.
>
> **La storia mia**
> My story
>
> **è breve. A tela o a seta**
> in short. I embroider linen or silk
>
> **ricamo in casa e fuori.**
> in my home and outside.
>
> **Son tranquilla e lieta**
> I'm contented and happy,

ed è mio svago
and enjoy

far giglie e rose.
making lilies and roses.

Mi piaccon quelle cose
I like those things

che han sì dolce malia,
that possess such sweet enchantment,

che parlano d'amor, di primavera,
that speak of love, of springtime,

che parlano di sogni e chimere—
that speak of dreams and fancies—

quelle cose che han nome poesia
those things called poetry.

Lei m'intende?
Do you understand me?

[Rodolfo: Sì.]
[Rodolfo: Yes.]

Mi chiamano Mimì,
They call me Mimì,

il perchè non so.
I don't know why.

Sola mi fo
I make

il pranzo da me stessa.
dinner for myself alone.

Non vado sempre a messa
I don't always go to Mass,

ma prego assai il Signor.
but I often pray to God.

Vivo sola, soletta,
I live alone, all alone,

là in una bianca cameretta:
in a little white room over there.

guardo su i tetti e in cielo,
I have a view over the roofs and into the sky,

ma quando vien lo sgelo
but when it thaws,

il primo sole è mio—
I get the first sunshine—

il primo bacio dell'aprile è mio!
April's first kiss is mine!

il primo sole è mio!
The first sunshine is mine!

Germoglia
Blooms

in un vaso una rosa.
a rose in a vase.

Foglia a foglia
Petal by petal

la spiro! Così gentil
I sniff it! How lovely

il profumo d'un fior!
is the fragrance of a flower!

Ma i fior ch'io faccio, ahimè,
But the flowers that I make, alas!

non hanno odore!
have no smell!

Altro di me non le saprei narrare:
I don't know what else to tell you about myself:

sono la tua vecina
I'm your neighbor

che la vien fuori d'ora
who comes to you at this late hour

a importunare.
to bother you.

VOCABULARY

Mi chiamano Mimì: They call me Mimì.
Mi chiamo Mimì: My name is Mimì.
Come si chiama? What is your name? (formal)
Come ti chiami? What is your name? (informal)

la tela: cloth, linen

la seta: silk
una camicia di seta: a silk blouse

lo svago: relaxation, pastime, amusement
l'hai fatto per svago: you did it just to pass the time
il giglio: lily
la rosa: rose

Mi piacciono quelle cose: I like those things (literally: these things are pleasing to me)

la malia: spell, charm
sono sotto la sua malia: I'm under her spell.

il tetto: roof, top, home
restare senza tetto: to be homeless (without a roof over one's head)

il profumo: perfume, scent
hai un buon profumo: you smell nice
questi fiori hanno un buon profumo: these flowers smell lovely

Quando men vo (Musetta, Act II)

Known as "Musetta's Waltz," this aria shows Musetta (a much showier woman than Mimì) trying to seduce an ex-lover, Marcello…

> **Quando men vo,**
> When I pass by,
>
> **quando men vo soletta per la via,**
> when I pass by alone on the street,
>
> **la gente sosta e mira,**
> people stop and stare,
>
> **e la bellezza mia tutta ricerca in me,**
> and examine all my beauty,
>
> **da capo a piè—**
> from head to foot—

[Marcello and Alcindoro each sing one line]

ed assaporo allor la bramosia
and then I relish the acute desire

sottil che dagl' occhi traspira
which they show in their eyes

e dai palesi vezzi intender sa
and which from the evident attractions can intuit

alle occulte beltà.

Così l'effluvio del desio
And so the outpouring of longing

tutta m'aggira,
surrounds me,

felice mi fa.
delights me!

VOCABULARY

da capo a piedi: from head to foot
era coperto di fango da capo a piedi: he was covered in mud from head to foot

la bramosia (di): longing (for), yearning (for)
se non arriva subito morirò di bramosia! If he does not come soon I will die of longing!

i vezzi: affected ways, charm

occulto, a: hidden, secret, concealed

la beltà: looks, beauty

il desio: desire

127

Donde lieta uscì (Mimì, Act III)

Mimì suggests to Rodolfo that they part as friends…

Donde lieta uscì al tuo grido
She lightheartedly left at your loving call

d'amore torna sola
she returns alone

Mimì al solitario nido.
Mimì to the solitary nest.

Ritorna un' altra volta
She returns once more

a intesser finti fior.
to weave artificial flowers.

Addio senza rancor.
Goodbye, with no hard feelings.

Ascolta, ascolta.
Listen, listen.

Le poche robe aduna che lasciai sparse.
Gather up the few things that I left scattered about.

Nel mio cassetto stan chiusi
Locked in my drawer

quel cherchietto d'or,
are the golden ring

e il libro di preghiere.
and my prayer book.

Involgi tutto quanto in un grembiale,
Wrap them all up in an apron,

manderò il portiere.
I'll send the porter round.

Bada—sotto il guanciale
Listen!—under the pillow

c'è la cuffietta rosa.
is the pink bonnet.

Se vuoi serbarla a ricordo d'amor!
You may want to save it as a memento of our love!

Addio, addio, senza rancor!
Goodbye, goodbye with no hard feelings!

VOCABULARY

il nido: nest
asilo nido: daycare center

senza rancor: with no hard feelings
il rancore: resentment
dimentichiamo i vecchi rancori: let bygones be bygones

la preghiera: prayer, request
È l'unica preghiera che ricordo: It's the only prayer I can remember

il grembiule: apron

il guanciale: pillow
dormire fra due guanciali: to sleep easy

la cuffietta: bonnet
la cuffia: bonnet, cap, headphones
la cuffia da bagno: shower cap

rosa: pink
stampa rosa: women's magazines
vedere tutto rosa: to see everything through rose-tinted glasses
un romanzo rosa: a romance novel

il ricordo: memory
ho dei bellissimi ricordi di Roma: I have very happy memories of
  Rome.
vivere di ricordi: to live in the past

l'amore: love, affection,
una canzone d'amore: a love song
amore libero: free love
amore di sé: egoism, selfishness
amor proprio: self-esteem, pride

addio: farewell
dire addio a qualcuno: to say goodbye to someone
addio al celibato: bachelor party

Vecchia zimarra (Colline, Act IV)

The philosopher Colline says goodbye to his beloved coat, which he
must pawn...

> **Vecchia zimarra, senti,**
> Listen, old overcoat,
>
> **io resto al pian,**
> I'm staying at ground level,

tu ascendere
you must now climb

il sacro monte or devi.
the sacred mountain. (slang for pawnshop)

Le mie grazie ricevi.
Accept my thanks.

Mai non curvasti il logoro
Never have you bent your threadbare

dorso ai ricchi ed ai potenti
back to the rich and to the powerful.

Passar nelle tue tasche
They have spent time in your pockets—

filosofi e poeti.
philosophers and poets.

Ora che i giorni lieti
Now that these happy days

fuggir, ti dico addio,
are gone, I bid you farewell,

fedele amico mio,
my faithful friend,

addio, addio.
Farewell, farewell.

VOCABULARY

logoro, a: worn out, threadbare, shabby
indossava un cappotto logoro: he was wearing a shabby overcoat

il dorso: back, spine, crest
a dorso di cavallo: on horseback
nuotare a dorso: to do the backstroke

la tasca: pocket
le tasche: pockets
l'ha messo nella tasca della giacca: he put it in his jacket pocket
Non ho un soldo in tasca: I don't have a penny on me
Conosco Roma come le mie tasche: I know Rome like my pockets (i.e., "the back of my hand").

il filosofo/la filosofa: philosopher
la filosofia: philosophy

In the last scene, Mimì dies of consumption.

La fanciulla del West (1910)

"The Girl of the Golden West" is Minnie, a bible-thumping cowgirl in a setting as exotic to Puccini as that of *Madama Butterfly*—the Wild West. Minnie is a woman in a bar full of homesick men who holds her own and manages to be both mother and sweetheart to them.

Oh, se sapeste come il vivere è allegro! (Minnie, Act II)

In this aria, she is expressing the joy she feels about her life—it's nothing fancy, but it suits her.

> **Oh, se sapeste come il vivere è allegro!**
> Oh, if you only knew how happy my life is!

Ho un piccolo polledro che me porta a
I have a little colt that takes me

galoppo laggiù per la compagna;
down there at a gallop

per prati di giunchiglie, di garofani ardenti,
down through the fields of daffodils, of red carnations,

per rivivere profunde cui profuman le sponde
and through deep shores whose banks are scented with

gelsomini e vainiglie!
jasmine and vanilla!

Poi ritorno ai miei pini ai monti della Sierra
Then I return to my pines and the hills of the Sierra

così al cielo vicini che Iddio pasando pare la
that are so close to Heaven that God passing by can almost

sua mano v'inclini,
touch them with His hand

lontani dalla terra così, che vien la voglia di
and it's so far away from the earth that I can almost

battere alla soglia del ciel per entrar!
knock at Heaven's threshold to enter!

VOCABULARY
la giunchiglia: daffodil
bella come una giunchiglia: pretty like a daffodil

il garofano: carnation
Posso prendere un mazzo di garofani? Can I take a bunch of carnations?

il fiore: flower
la margherita: daisy
la rosa: rose
la viola: violet
il tulipano: tulip
il lillà: lilac

l'albero: tree
l'abete: fir tree
il cipresso: cypress
il pino: pine
la quercia: oak
il sughero: cork oak

il gelsomino: jasmine
mi piace il té al gelsomino: I like Jasmine tea.

la vaniglia: vanilla
un gelato alla vaniglia: a vanilla ice cream

Una parola sola (Johnson, Act II)

Here the handsome stranger Johnson reveals that he is the wanted man Ramerrez, and he asks Minnie to let him explain himself.

> **Una parola sola!**
> Let me have just one word!
>
> **Non mi difenderò sono un dannato!**
> I won't defend myself. I'm a cursed man!

Lo so, lo so!
I know it, I know it!

Ma non vi avrei rubato!
But I wouldn't have robbed you!

Sono Ramerrez, nacqui vagabondo:
I'm Ramerrez, I was born a vagabond:

era ladro il mio nome da quando venni al mondo.
my name was thief from the moment I came into the world.

Ma finchè visse mio padre, io non sapevo.
But while my father lived, I didn't know it.

Or son sei mesi che mio padre morì.
Now it's six months since my father died.

Solo ricchezza mia, per la madre e pei fratelli, alle dimane,
My only wealth, for my mother, for my brothers, for the future

l'eredità paterna una masnada di bandito di strada!
was my father's inheritance: a gang of highway bandits!

L'accettai!
I accepted it!

Era quello il mio destino!
It was my destiny!

Ma un giorno v'ho incontrata.
But one day I met you.

Ho sognato d'andarmene coi voi tanto
I dreamed of going away with you

lontano e redimermi tutto in una vita di lavoro e d'amore.
far away and totally redeem myself in a life of work and love.

E il labbro mio mormorò un'ardente preghiera:
And my lips murmured an impassioned prayer:

Oh Dio! Ch'ella non sappia mai la mia vergogna!
Oh God! May she never know my shame!

Ahimè! Ahimè! Vergogna mia!
Alas! Alas! My shame!

Il sogno è stato vano!
My dream has been in vain!

Ora ho finito!
Now I'm finished!

VOCABULARY
la parola: speech, word
rimanere senza parole: to be speechless
È una parola! It's easier said than done!

dannato: damned
quella dannata macchina! that damned car!
i dannati: the damned

lo so: I know (it)

la ricchezza: wealth, richness
le ricchezze naturali: natural resources

ladro: thief
al ladro! Stop, thief!
l'occasione fa l'uomo ladro: opportunity makes the thief

vergogna: shame
È arrosito per la vergogna: he went red with embarrassment
provo vergogna davanti a lui: he makes me feel shy
Credevo di morire per la vergogna! I thought I'd die of shame of it!

Ch'ella mi creda libero e lontano (Johnson, Act III)

About to be hanged, Johnson begs his captors to lie to Minnie and tell her he is "free and far away."

Ch'ella mi creda libero e lontano,
I want her to believe that I'm free and far away,

sopra una nuova via di redenzione!
on a new path of redemption!

Aspetterà ch'io torni.
She'll be waiting for me to return.

E passeranno i giorni ed io non tornerò.
The days will pass and I won't return.

Minnie, che m'hai voluto tanto bene!
Minnie, who has loved me so much!

Ah! Tu della mia vita mio solo fior!
Ah! You are the only flower in my life!

VOCABULARY
libero: free
Sei libera domani sera? Are you free tomorrow evening?
È libero questo posto? Is this seat free?

lontano: distant, faraway
Il mare non è lontano da qui: The sea isn't far from here
Abiti lontano dalla scuola? Do you live far from school?

via: road, street, path, away, out
Abito in una via molto stretta: I live on a very narrow street.
Buttare/gettare via: to throw something away
Vai via! Go away!

aspettare: to wait for
posso aspettare: I can wait
Mi ha fatto aspettare un'ora: he kept me waiting for an hour

M'hai voluto tanto bene! You loved me so much!
volersi bene: to love each other
E lo dico perché ti voglio bene: And I'm saying this because I love you.
Ti voglio bene e mi dispiace: I love you and I'm sorry.

Conclusion

I hope this book has ignited your interest in both Italian and opera. Of course, there is no substitute for actual practice with conversation. And please seek out recordings of the operas excerpted in this book.

It's true that when you are at the opera, the words are hard to follow whatever language they're in. That's why it's so important to know the libretto and arrive at the opera house prepared. Do your homework!

What's more, some of the words in the operas we covered are outdated. I've focused on the vocabulary that makes sense in the present day.

In the end, opera is the perfect art form. Some call it elitist, but it appeals to all the senses on a basic—if magical—level. What starts out as a punishing experience of hearing "the fat lady sing" becomes an all-encompassing passion that—like Don Giovanni's appetite—can never be satisfied. We keep coming back because that is where we are our true selves. Just as I understood as an anxious child, there's nothing like the awe-inspiring freedom of dwelling in an audience.

BIBLIOGRAPHY

General References

Abbate, Carolyn, and Roger Parker. *A History of Opera*. New York: W.W. Norton & Company, Inc., 2012.

Smith, Peter Fox. *A Passion for Opera*. North Pomfret, Vermont: Trafalgar Square Publishing, 2004.

Snowman, Daniel. *The Gilded Stage: A Social History of Opera*. London: Atlantic Books, 2009.

Plotkin, Fred. *Opera 101*. New York: Hyperion, 1994.

Chapter One: Handel

Hogwood, Christopher. *Handel*. New York: Thames & Hudson Inc, 2007.

Keates, Jonathan. *Handel: The Man & His Music*. London: Pimlico, 2009.

Chapter Two: Mozart

Bolt, Rodney. *The Librettist of Venice: The Remarkable Life of Lorenzo Da Ponte*. New York: Bloomsbury Publishing, 2006.

Glover, Jane. *Mozart's Women: His Family, His Friends, His Music*. New York: HarperCollins Publishers, 2006.

Gutman, Robert W. *Mozart: A Cultural Biography*. Orlando, Florida: Harcourt, Inc., 1999.

Johnson, Paul. *Mozart: A Life*. New York: Penguin Books, 2013.

Chapter Three: Rossini
Servadio, Gaia. *Rossini.* New York: Carroll & Graf Publishers, 2003.

Chapter Four: Donizetti
Weinstock, Herbert. *Donizetti and the World of Opera in Italy, Paris and Vienna in the First Half of the Nineteenth Century.* New York: Pantheon Books, 1963.

Chapter Five: Bellini
Galatopoulos, Stelios. *Bellini: Life, Times, Music.* London: Sanctuary Publishing Limited, 2002.

Chapter Six: Verdi
Berger, William. *Verdi with a Vengeance.* New York: Vintage Books, 2000.

Chapter Seven: Pucchini
Berger, William. *Puccini Without Excuses.* New York: Vintage Books, 2005.

Made in the USA
Coppell, TX
07 October 2022

84232477R00079